P|
FRO]

MW01233675

"Joel Comiskey's concept of 'G-12.3' may be what God will use to help you and your church move into a mighty harvest. That is the desire of the author. Celebrate with me his clarity and recommendations."

RALPH W. NEIGHBOUR, JR.
FOUNDER, TOUCH OUTREACH MINISTRIES

"As a missionary, I have been waiting for this book. It is a contextualized approach to G-12, and it will be a great resource for the Cell Church Movement."

LAURENCE SINGLEHURST
DIRECTOR, CELL UK MINISTRIES

"Our human tendency is to think that if we can just find the right model for doing church, we will become successful. Rather than presenting G-12.3 as a 'secret formula' to follow, Joel Comiskey provides practical insight in how to effectively adapt G-12 principles rather than to simply adopt a particular G-12 model. This is a 'must read' for leaders who desire to implement the G-12 strategy while at the same time remaining faithful to the unique plan God had given them to fulfill."

GERALD E. MARTIN
CORNERSTONE CHURCH & MINISTRIES INTERNATIONAL

"Joel Comiskey is clearly one of the leading thinkers and writers on the Cell Church Movement around the world. In this book, Joel does a excellent job of further explaining the principles of the 'G-12 model' and how they can be applied wisely to each unique church and ministry."

MARK CONNER
SENIOR MINISTER, WAVERLY CHRISTIAN FELLOWSHIP

"To every pastor who cannot 'adopt' ICM's model of the G-12, here is a creative approach to adapting the successful principles that have made ICM and other churches successful. Joel Comiskey cites many examples of how, once these principles are implemented, any church can experience growth in discipleship and evangelism. The G-12.3 is a very workable model for modern America. I believe in the 'Principle of Twelve' but know from years of ministry that it must constantly evolve to keep up with what God is doing on the earth as new cultural trends emerge."

BILLY HORNSBY
DIRECTOR OF THE ASSOCIATION OF RELATED CHURCHES

"In this book, Joel Comiskey introduces the next important piece of the dialogue concerning the G-12 cell church: principles. In Chapter One, Comiskey establishes the necessity of understanding the G-12 model from its underlying roots. This book will help readers grasp the G-12 principles that are necessary to understand current models and implement the G-12 structure or a modification of it, such as Comiskey's G-12.3."

BILL BECKHAM
DIRECTOR, TOUCH GLOBAL

"Joel Comiskey has the heartbeat of what is happening in the cell church around the world. He clearly communicates G-12 principles and explains how to make them work in various local settings. This practical guide will prove invaluable for any G-12 strategy."

LARRY KREIDER
DIRECTOR, DOVE CHRISTIAN FELLOWSHIP INTERNATIONAL

"God has worked through Joel Comiskey to help many cell church pastors throughout the world. Pastors in Korea have found great insight and wisdom through Joel's books. I have been waiting for this new book for a long time—every cell church pastor should be handed this book! I pray that the G-12.3 vision as it is presented here will edify and multiply the Kingdom of God everywhere."

PAUL JEONG
PRESIDENT, TOUCH KOREA

FROM 12 TO 3

FROM 12 TO 3

HOW TO APPLY G-12 PRINCIPLES IN YOUR CHURCH

JOEL COMISKEY

TOUCH PUBLICATIONS
Houston, Texas, U.S.A.

Published by TOUCH Publications
P.O. Box 19888
Houston, Texas, 77224-9888, U.S.A.
(281) 497-7901 • Fax (281) 497-0904

Cover design by Don Bleyl
Editing by Scott Boren and Brandy Egli

International Standard Book Number: 1-880828-41-3

TOUCH Publications is the book-publishing division
of TOUCH Outreach Ministries, a resource and consulting
ministry for churches with a vision for cell-based local
church structure.

Find us on the World Wide Web at
http://www.touchusa.org

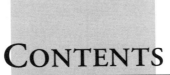

CONTENTS

FOREWORD

As a young pastor, Yonggi Cho received a vision from God to commission Christians to become cell group leaders. He created cell church patterns through many years of trial and error, floundering for a number of years until he found the best pattern for Korea. His cells then doubled, and doubled again. At present, Pastor Cho shepherds the largest church in the world and supports missionaries all over the Earth. The phenomenal growth Yoido Full Gospel Church experienced came after much prayer, testing, and Spirit-given guidance. We can observe the results YFGC has had because it is now in its fourth decade. The growth is largely through conversions.

Many pastors, including myself, followed Pastor Cho's pattern of structuring cell groups as "Basic Christian Communities." The Korean pattern is called the "Five by Five" structure for managing cell groups. I learned it and applied it in Singapore, where I worked with Faith Community Baptist Church and watched it grow from around 600 members to over 7,000 in a period of five years. FCBC's cell life was very different from that of the cells at YFGC. Cell members at YFGC focused on Bible study and Pastor Cho taught the "lessons" to the cell leaders himself. YFGC added fellowship and evangelism to the cell meetings, and it was appropriate for Korean culture. At FCBC, Biblical teaching took place during our Sunday services and cell group meetings focused on edification. The management systems were the same, but cell life was very different. Our conversion rate was five people per day, month in and month out.

Dion Robert, senior pastor of the Works and Mission Baptist Church in the Ivory Coast listened to a reading of Pastor Cho's book, *More Than Numbers*, caught the principles, and formed his cells in an African culture that is filled with animistic demon possession. This culture requires cell groups to minister to the deep needs of demonized people. In twenty years, Pastor Robert grew his church to over 120,000 members. Unlike the churches in Korea and Singapore, his central complex of buildings includes a 24-hour-a-day clinic for casting out demons. His management structure is nothing like Pastor Cho's. Few have sought to implement it outside of the Ivory Coast, but the Works and Mission has branches in France, Denmark, and 18 other nations.

In El Salvador, another pastor examined the Korean model and adjusted it to his Central American republic. At Elim church, they conduct two cell meetings each week: one for edification and one for evangelism. The present pastor replaced the founder, but the cell groups, managed by a "Five by Five" structure, have never slowed down. Elim has penetrated the entire nation and is even spreading all over the world, numbering 120,000 in the mother church. The cell structure was not built on the powerful personality of a man, but on the principle of equipping all believers to evangelize. Although Pastor Vega mentors his churches carefully, they work best in a Latin American culture.

In recent years, another form of cell management has developed in Bogota, Colombia. Formed in the hearts of César and Claudia Castellanos, the system, organized on a "Principle of Twelve," was largely developed with the assistance of César Fajardo and his wife. This new pattern has captivated many people in many nations. As reported in this book, the development of the International Charismatic Mission is one of moist clay being molded and shaped to harvest in a Latin American community.

Dr. Joel Comiskey has reported on the progress of that movement throughout this book. We pray God's richest blessings upon César and Claudia Castellanos, who were entrusted with the "Principle of Twelve." It may be exactly right for you, and if so, they are happy to take you in hand and direct you as you implement their strategy. They strongly mentor all who intend to adopt it. Remember, however, that for many years they were adapting, revising, and changing the vision so rapidly that they did not want to put into print what they were doing. When clay is wet and not yet hardened by the years, it can be continually reshaped and adjusted. The "Principle of Twelve" is now official; books are being written about the patterns César and Claudia Castellanos have created.

Dr. Comiskey, the author of this book, has sought to pay great respect to the "mother church" of the "Principle of Twelve." As he absorbed it through many trips to ICM, he saw ways it needed to be tweaked or improved to be appropriate to the ministry he was developing in Ecuador. His presentation, chapter by chapter, leaves you free to either completely adopt the "pure" G-12 model, or to consider the ways it can be adjusted to fit specific issues. His concept of "G-12.3" may be what God will use to help you and your church move into a mighty harvest. That is the desire of the author. Celebrate with me his clarity and recommendations.

Ralph W. Neighbour, Jr.
Houston, Texas

INTRODUCTION

One pastor who struggled with his cell church recently came back from a G-12 conference saying, "I was a blind man without vision before the conference. Now I can see, and what I see excites me; we are pressing on with what God has put on our hearts...in Bogota, they believe and hold on to the values one hundred percent! They really believe everyone has the potential to be a leader. They really believe that everyone can be a spiritual parent."[1] Many churches are seeing the G-12 care structure as a breath of fresh air. There is a grass-roots power to it that brings ministry down to where people live, work, and breathe.

The G-12 vision is spreading. Bethany World Prayer Center, one of the most prominent cell churches in the U.S., has decided to fully implement the G-12 model. Faith Community Baptist Church (FCBC) in Singapore has also decided to commit to the G-12 model. During their February 2002 G-12 conference with Pastor Castellanos, FCBC officially 'dismantled' the geographical organization of cells according to districts. Just like Bethany World Prayer Center, they are now using a system of homogeneous networks. FCBC's senior pastor, Lawrence Khong, has a vision to plant one hundred thousand cells in the next ten years.[2] Pastor Khong gave the following reasons for the change to the G-12 structure:

- G-12 provides a system for long-term relationships and leadership training.
- Evangelism is disciple-making, not just a one-time event.
- Homogeneous groups are stronger than geographical groups.
- Every person can lead a cell group.

Colin Dye, pastor of the 10,000 member Kensington Temple Church in London, England, is fully committed to the G-12 strategy. He believes that every church should follow the G-12 vision.[3] He says, "It represents for us today the restoration of true apostolic and governmental authority and spiritual effectiveness to the body of Christ on earth."[4]

Most likely your church also needs a jump-start. I believe that you can fine-tune your cell church vision with the G-12 strategy. But I want this book to be more than a quick-fix. My prayer is that it will clarify your questions and help you to take the next step in your cell church transition.

WHY ANOTHER BOOK ON G-12?

My first book, *Groups of Twelve: A New Way to Mobilize Leaders and Multiply Groups in your Church* (TOUCH Publications, 1999), described what was happening at the International Charismatic Mission in Bogota, Colombia. It elaborated on the key G-12 principles, and what churches are doing to apply those principles. I would recommend that you read my first G-12 book if you seek to gain a foundational understanding of the subject.

This current book will take you beyond the last one. I am writing this current book for two major reasons.

The First Book Was More Descriptive

The first book was an in-depth case study of ICM in Bogota, Colombia. The first six chapters described ICM's vision, values, cell groups, G-12 system, training track, and multiplication success.[5]

I am writing this book because some readers stopped after Chapter 6 and thought I was prescribing ICM's model, when in reality I was encouraging application of the principles that the second part of the book emphasized. Some people felt I was promoting the need to adopt the entire G-12 package. Consider one person's response to my first G-12 book:

> About six years ago, our church moved from PBD [program based design] toward cells and implemented 5x5. After struggling with that format, our pastor began looking for something more for us. He encouraged cell leaders to read your book and eventually that 'system' was adopted exactly as it was from the first half of the book, and the leadership struggled to move our cells into that direction…The first six chapters of your book describe how ICM has organized and the rest of your book provides wisdom about what can be learned from ICM and applied in other places (the principles)…how many people do you know read only the first half of the instructions and think they have it?[6]

This book is not a description of ICM or how to implement its exact model. Many churches are already doing that. This book is designed to help you to implement the guiding principles of G-12 to your unique church situation.

My Evolution with G-12 Principles

My understanding of the G-12 system has evolved since I wrote the last book; I have learned so many new, practical lessons since then that I felt compelled to write them down.

My journey toward understanding the G-12 model first began in 1975, when I began leading my first cell group. Each week, friends and family gathered to apply Scripture. In 1983, I planted a church in downtown Long Beach, California and implemented Pastor Cho's cell group philosophy based on his success at Yoido Full Gospel Church in Seoul, Korea. In 1991, as a missionary in Quito, Ecuador, I began a cell group ministry among university students at El Batan Church that exploded to include the rest of the church. In 1994, my wife and I, along with two pastors from El Batan Church, planted a cell-based church in Quito called the Republic Church.

From 1995-1997, I wrote my doctoral thesis on the cell church movement worldwide, which included ICM. In 1996, as part of my research, I spent ten days living inside ICM in an extra room they converted into an apartment for visitors. That first visit initiated a yearly pilgrimage to ICM to learn their principles so that I could introduce others to the G-12 concept.

In 1997, I returned to the church I had co-founded in Quito to help give direction to a new cell church vision. The Republic Church exploded to over 275 cell groups and 1300 people attending cells. In 2000, I left the pastoral team and began to minister to other churches in Quito to help them make the cell church transition. Since I was living and working in Ecuador as a missionary with the Christian and Missionary Alliance, I had ample opportunity to apply what I first saw at ICM.

The Republic Church invited members of Pastor Castellanos G-12 group to minister in our church and give advice. Even so, we were not content with copying someone else's model. We wrestled with how to apply G-12 principles in our context. We wanted to develop our own G-12 vision.

My family and I recently helped start a cell church in Southern California, and I am coaching five additional pastors in the Southern California area who are transitioning to the cell church model. In each of the churches with whom I am currently consulting, I have discovered the need to apply G-12 principles in a slightly different way because each church has a distinct culture and each church is at a different place in its journey.[7]

These differences made me realize the need to adapt G-12 principles to unique environments. One size does not fit all. No two churches are exactly the same, and thus each requires a different starting point and different methods.

I believe strongly in G-12 principles, but I am first and foremost an advocate of the cell church. First I encourage churches to become cell churches, then I teach them to fine-tune their cell church experiences through G-12 principles.

From these G-12 principles, I have developed a cell church structure that I call the G-12.3, which will be fully explained in Chapter 3. Such a structure has proven to provide more flexibility in various settings. I developed this adapted G-12 structure while working with the pastoral team in Ecuador. Subsequently, I have helped many churches small and large apply G-12 principles through the use of the G-12.3.

G-12 TERMINOLOGY

Most of the initial confusion about G-12 groups comes from the terminology. I think it is always better to use a phrase that gives immediate clarity, rather than one that demands a definition.[8]

- G-12: a team of cell leaders. I would encourage you, in fact, to use 'team gathering' or 'leadership group' instead of G-12 group.
- Cell Group: a group of 4-15 people that meets weekly outside the church building for the purpose of evangelism and discipleship with the goal of multiplication.
- Cell Church: a church driven by cell groups and where celebration and cell are equally important.
- ICM: the International Charismatic Mission, located in Bogota, Colombia. This is the cell church that originated the G-12 leadership care structure.
- Pastor César Castellanos: the founding pastor of ICM and the person who initially received the G-12 vision.
- YFGC: Yoido Full Gospel Church, located in Seoul, Korea. This church is the largest church in the world and grew that way through cell groups.
- Pastor Yonggi Cho: the senior pastor of YFGC and the person who originally received the cell church vision and creator of the 5x5 model of leadership care.

How the Book Is Structured

This book is divided into four major sections. Chapters 1 through 5 explain how to apply the G-12 model in a simple and understandable way. This section will define the G-12 strategy and help both pastors and lay leaders to apply it. Section Two, Chapters 6 through 8, examines key values of the G-12 strategy, including prayer, Encounter Retreats, and the belief that everyone can facilitate a cell group. The third section, consisting of Chapters 9 through 11, lays out the practical nuts and bolts of the G-12 strategy, explaining homogenous networks, G-12 material, and the G-12 meeting. The fourth and final section, Chapters 12 and 13, applies G-12.3

principles to a wide variety of churches and church situations. There is also an appendix, in which you will find sample G-12 lessons.

There are several different ways that this book can be used:

1. Start at the beginning and read the entire book to gain a complete understanding of how to use and apply G-12 principles in your church.
2. Skip to the chapter or chapters that address the areas where your church needs specific development. For example, if you are confused about how to apply G-12 principles or the G-12.3 strategy in a particular stage of development, skip to Chapters 12 and 13.
3. Read through the book with other leaders and coaches and discuss what you are learning.

MAKING SENSE
OF THE G-12 SYSTEM

1

G-12 PRINCIPLES
OR G-12 MODEL?

The G-12 strategy has become a powerful tool to refine the cell church worldwide. The amazing growth of ICM in Bogota, Colombia has generated a great deal of excitement because of the simple yet powerful strategy God gave them. If and when this excitement moves a church to respond, that church typically follows one of two paths:

- It follows the entire G-12 model.

Current examples of this approach are Harvest Assembly in Virginia Beach, Virginia, the Christian Center in Guayaquil, Ecuador, Kensington Temple Church in England, and Bethany World Prayer Center in Baker, Louisiana. These churches follow the G-12 model in its entirety, exactly like ICM does.

- It applies the guiding G-12 principles.

Examples abound of churches that have chosen to follow G-12 principles, rather than to adopt the entire model. In my last G-12 book, I dedicated two chapters to highlighting twelve case-study churches. Of those twelve, ten adapted the G-12 strategy to their particular situations, applying the underlying principles rather than the entire model. Two examples I did not include in my previous book are Cypress Creek Church in Wimberley, Texas and Liverpool Christian Life Centre in Liverpool, Australia.

THE MODEL APPROACH

Some churches have chosen to follow the entire ICM model. This approach is summed up by pastor Larry Stockstill, who, when talking about the G-12 model, said:

> If you try to Americanize everything, it will not work. There is no reason whatsoever to alter what you see. We've been around that mountain for a long time. There is no reason to alter what you see in the Word and in the pattern. As you implement, you will immediately see the results of it. If you don't, you're not going to see any results.[1]

Bethany has felt the Lord's leading to align themselves with ICM and follow its exact configuration, training track, emphasis on twelve as God's chosen number, and care structure.[2] God is blessing Bethany in an amazing way and helping them to reap the harvest like never before.[3]

Harvest Assembly in Virginia Beach, Virginia is another church that has followed the G-12 model in its entirety. One of the staff members said, "We understand that we must accept the whole package, that we cannot pick and choose."[4] Mike Osborn, the youth pastor, has made over thirteen trips to ICM, vacationed personally with Pastor Castellanos, and received step-by-step counsel on how to proceed. Harvest Assembly uses the exact same Encounter Retreats, School of Leadership, and follow-up system as ICM.

The Christian Center of Guayaquil, Ecuador (CCG) faithfully followed the classic 5x5 model developed by Pastor Cho and had grown to become the largest church in Ecuador. Even so, when Pastor Jerry Smith witnessed the explosive growth at ICM, he decided to adopt the G-12 model. CCG has sent over 50 pastors and leaders to ICM in order to understand the G-12 model and then implement it back home.

CCG asks all its cell leaders to commit themselves to three meetings per week. Each cell leader meets with his or her G-12 leader (first meeting), meets with his own G-12 members (second meeting), and leads an open cell group (third meeting), just as they do at ICM. CCG has also patterned its leadership training on ICM's. It holds similar Encounter retreats and its School of Leaders is identical, lasting nine months and having three trimesters.[5] CCG changed radically in order to to embrace ICM's G-12 model.

The Metro Church International, located in Sunderland, England, is led by Ken and Lois Gott. This is also an ICM-model G-12 church. In 1998, Pastors Ken and Lois met Pastor Castellanos at the Assembly of God national conference in Prestatyn, Wales and he challenged them to dismiss the crowds in order to build the church through disciple-making. This they did, and from that time onward began the transition into G-12. Pastor Ken is now a member of Pastor Castellanos' International Group of Twelve and travels to Colombia twice each year to meet with Pastor Castellanos and the other members of his G-12.[6]

In Chile, the IPETRI, an independent Pentecostal church, represents ICM. Senior Pastor José Rivas identifies himself as a member of the International Group of Twelve of Pastor Castellanos.

He wrote in a conference brochure, "One of the first things we learned in the vision was: you must adopt; not adapt. We must not forget this premise. To adapt the vision reveals pride, vanity, and self-sufficiency. Pastor Castellanos says this: 'why should we try to re-invent the wheel, when it's already been invented?' He is right."[7]

Those churches who choose to follow this approach usually:

- Establish a covenant relationship with ICM to follow the G-12 system in its entirety. More recently, ICM has asked people to sign a written agreement to follow ICM's system exactly. This written agreement allows churches to use ICM's material.
- Follow the exact same training track, which includes—
  - Pre-encounter
  - Encounter Retreat
  - Post-encounter
  - School of Leaders
- Promote the number twelve as God's special number.
- Become part of the ICM network of churches, which normally requires multiple trips to Bogota each year.

Some churches will follow the ICM model in its entirety and do it successfully. These churches are sold on the G-12 vision, and believe that God has anointed ICM in a special way and thus willingly submit to ICM's covering.

If you choose to follow this path, you may want to visit an ICM-model G-12 church and read the literature that promotes this approach (e.g., Rocky Malloy's *Groups of Twelve: Launching your Ministry into Explosive Growth*, Pastor César Castellanos' book *Leadership of Success through the Group of 12*, and the first six chapters of my book *Groups of Twelve*.)[8]

CAUTIONS OF THE MODEL APPROACH

Be Prepared to Adapt

We must always remember that Pastor Castellanos and his team at ICM have reached their current success by constantly adapting. ICM began its ministry by completely following Pastor Cho's cell system. For example, ICM organized small groups geographically throughout Bogota, just like Pastor Cho did at YFGC, and they used the 5x5 care structure.

As Pastor Castellanos reflected, however, he acknowledged that the early system needed fine-tuning because he had failed to adapt it to his own cultural context. ICM plodded along from 1986 to 1991, hoping for success but sensing that something was missing. Their cells grew, but they grew very slowly. By the end of 1991, there were only 70 cell groups.

It was in 1991 that Pastor Castellanos heard from God about G-12 principles and began to adjust his cell system to meet his church's unique needs. Since that time, ICM has been changing continuously. I have witnessed startling, radical changes from 1996-2002, having personally visited most of those years.

Normally, the founder of any given model understands the principles and values behind the model. There is complete liberty to change the model when the need arises. Those who follow the one model completely, on the other hand, often do not possess the same creativity.

I believe, in fact, that if you copy someone else's model in its entirety, there is the danger of always being several steps behind, which will force you to play 'catch-up.' For example, if you try to copy ICM's model exactly, what will you do when they change it? Will you go back to ICM and learn each new adjustment? In this situation, it becomes even more difficult because they come from a different culture and in most cases speak a different language.

You need to be sensitive to your church context, to where you are in your transition, and to the receptivity of your church members. Trying to place an entire model over your church could be disastrous, especially if it does not fit properly.

The Latest Anointing

We have a tendency as pastors to follow the latest anointing, the latest church growth model. One pastor believes that ICM had a special ability to transfer God's anointing to others and this explains their success. He encouraged pastors to get under their 'anointing,' so that it might trickle down to them.

But, is it so simple? One cell church pastor described the current situation like this:

> We in Europe and North America, who are struggling with being successful, might believe that if we only will find the right thing, we will have the breakthrough that we so badly desire and that we see happening in other parts of the world. This creates some kind of 'wave-hopping.' From Power Evangelism to Willow Creek to spiritual mapping to Toronto Blessing to Cell Church to G-12. The hope is that the next wave may just be 'it.' After the initial excitement fades and the results are less than expected, we can be sure that the next wave will come around to save us. I am excited about G-12 principles. And attending a conference with César Castellanos was one of the most blessed experiences for me. We are using G-12 principles in our new church plant in Germany. This, in my opinion, is one the greatest strengths of G-12. Reducing it to one closed model that you have to follow as an exact blueprint (because we hope this finally will be 'it' and will solve all our problems) is to lose one of the greatest strengths

that we have in G-12. I am completely sold on cell church, and I am excited about G-12. However, what really matters are New Testament values and principles. I believe very strongly that Jesus and the values and principles of His kingdom should be our focus. If we focus on models and waves, we will get sidetracked.[9]

Like Larry Kreider said, "We must fervently pray that our visions and goals are birthed by the Holy Spirit, not copied from the latest church appearing to be successful."[10]

As I have studied cell churches around the world, I have noticed that many follow specific foundational principles, common to all, while adapting those principles to each individual context.

THE PRINCIPLE-ORIENTED APPROACH

I teach cell seminars around the world and impart G-12 principles under the cell church strategy.[11] My ongoing burden is to find cell church principles that apply in any culture, so I am eager to accept the best G-12 principles within the cell church strategy. The whole cell church philosophy has united the body of Christ across different cultures and denominations. We have been able to network with one another, encourage one another, and learn from one another.

I received an e-mail from a church representative leader who had previously invited me to speak at his church but then changed his mind, deciding that he would not have me come speak at his cell seminar after all. He wrote: "The primary reason is in the last couple of months that we have been chatting we have decided to move aggressively towards a G-12 model and really consider the impact that has on our church. That being the case we feel that any presentation of the cell model of ministry may be a touch premature for us."[12]

I wrote him back saying: "I was just wondering how you differentiate the G-12 model from the cell model. Are you saying they're two different models? If so, where did you pick up that they're not the same?"

Perhaps the general confusion has come from the misconception that cell church meant following a particular oversight and support structure—like Pastor Cho's 5x5 model that is organized around geography. If this was ever true, it was only because of the lack of alternative oversight structures.

It is worth remembering that cell churches that follow geographical oversight structures have also grown very rapidly.[13] The 5x5 model that originated with Pastor Cho's church in Korea catapulted that church to become the largest church in the history of Christianity. Dion Robert, senior pastor of the Works and Mission Baptist Church in Abidjan, Ivory Coast, developed his own oversight and support structure and grew to 120,000 members, with 21 other nations touched by their missionary teams.

The Elim Church in San Salvador, El Salvador, adapted the 5x5 model by adding two meetings a week: one for cell members only and the other to reach out evangelistically as a normal cell group. This model has produced a church of 120,000 members in a small nation.

APPLYING G-12 PRINCIPLES

Most cell churches that admire the G-12 model take the best G-12 principles and apply them to their individual settings. I will be highlighting G-12 principles throughout this book, as well as churches who have done an excellent job applying them. Those churches following G-12 principles—as opposed to the entire model—are too numerous to name. They have each discovered fresh ways to fine-tune their cell-based churches by using G-12 principles and values. Churches that follow the principle-oriented approach are primarily concerned with becoming better cell churches and are excited about how certain principles or values of the G-12 approach can make this work.

The dictionary describes a principle as "an important underlying law or assumption required in a system of thought." The cell church movement, for example, believes the principle that the cell is just as important as the celebration and that both of them must be equally emphasized. This principle comes from the New Testament church. The early church celebrated together in large temple gatherings and then met from house to house (Acts 2:42-46; 5:42; 20:20). Later, due to persecution, this pattern became nearly impossible and the house church movement became the standard (Acts 12:12; Romans 16: 3-5; 1 Corinthians 16:19; Colossians 4:15; Philemon 2). Although we do not have many specific details about how the New Testament cell approach looked, the principle of cell-celebration guides our thinking.

We must humbly admit that none of the current cell church models are perfect. I would not state that Pastor Cho (Seoul, Korea), Pastor Neighbour (Houston, TX), Pastor Vega (San Salvador, El Salvador), Pastor Stockstill (Baker, LA), Pastor Robert (Abidjan, Ivory Coast), Pastor Daugherty (Tulsa, OK), or Pastor Castellanos (Bogota, Colombia) uses the only true, biblical cell church model. The pattern, or principle, is cell-celebration. The application of the cell church for today is varied and changes from culture to culture and church to church.

The same could be said of the New Testament teaching on worship. Paul did not promote only one model of worship. Rather, he laid down guiding principles for worship in the house of God. Paul said that when someone spoke in tongues, there should be an interpreter (1 Corinthians 14:13) and that spiritual gifts should be exercised in an orderly fashion (1 Corinthians 14:26-32). Paul's instructions were broad enough to apply to a variety of circumstances. Paul set forth principles, rather than promoting exact models.

Church government is another example. I do not believe there is one perfect church government model (e.g., Presbyterian, Congregational, combination, etc.). Paul, rather, gave principles or characteristics upon which to base the choice of leadership in the church (1 Timothy 3: 1-7; Titus 3), but Paul did not write down step by step instructions on how to run a church.

You are reading this book because you want to know how to do cell church better. My advice is to follow the common patterns or principles of the major cell churches. In my book *Reap the Harvest* (TOUCH Publications, 1999), I catalogued common principles and patterns found in all of the fastest growing worldwide cell churches. These principles include—

- Dependence on Jesus Christ through prayer.
- Senior pastor giving strong, visionary leadership to the cell ministry.
- Cell ministry promoted as the backbone of the church.
- A clear definition of a cell group (weekly, outside the church building, evangelistic, pastoral care/discipleship, clear goal of multiplication.)
- The passion behind cell ministry is evangelism and church growth.
- Reproduction (multiplication) is the major goal of each cell group.
- Cell and celebration attendance expected of everyone attending the church.
- Clearly established leadership requirements for those entering cell ministry.
- Required cell leadership training for all potential cell group leaders.
- Cell leadership developed from within the church itself, at all levels.
- A supervisory care structure for each level of leadership (G-12, 5x5, or something else.)

- Cell leadership promoted to higher leadership positions based on past success.
- Follow-up system of visitors and new converts administered through cell groups.
- Cell lessons based on pastor's teaching to promote continuity between cell and celebration (although flexibility might be given to meet specific homogeneous groups.)

In later chapters, I will be amplifying several crucial G-12 principles, such as:

- Everyone can become a cell leader.
- Every leader can disciple and supervise other leaders.
- People need to be set free (liberated from strongholds) in order to serve as harvest workers.
- A clear training track must immediately follow the Encounter Retreat.
- There must be fervent prayer and total commitment to Jesus Christ.

It is upon these principles that I base the G-12.3 structure. The key is not found in the specific structure that a church adopts, but in the principles that drive that structure. Without a clear understanding of basic cell church principles, the structure will only be a lifeless skeleton. The cell church strategy will constantly need refinement and adaptation to improve its overall quality and effectiveness. G-12 principles help us refine the cell church strategy—not replace it.

2

TEAMS

OF LEADERS

An excited couple sat in the front row of my cell seminar in Buenos Aires, Argentina. Before I even started my seminar, the man exclaimed, "We're a G-12 church." I could tell that he was excited about the church's new direction, especially because he had been specifically sent to the seminar by the senior pastor. He continued, "We used to be a cell church, but now we've decided to become a G-12 church."

"Oh really," I said. "What did you do to change from a cell church to a G-12 church?"

"Well," he said, "we decided to divide our entire congregation into groups of twelve people for the purpose of discipleship. My pastor is meeting with me and a few others, and I'll continue the process when I find my twelve." This pastor, like many others, thought that G-12 groups replaced multiplying open cell groups. He, like many pastors before him, heard about the new G-12 model and quickly applied the little knowledge he possessed.

As I co-taught the week-long seminar in Argentina, this leader began to understand how the G-12 care system complimented the cell structure, providing the means to disciple the cell leaders more effectively. In the seminar, I did not even talk about the actual G-12 oversight structure until the last session, although my entire seminar was filled with G-12 principles. He became aware that the G-12 oversight structure could not be separate from the cell church. Rather, it helped the cell church to become more effective.

I have discovered that the most common confusion in the G-12 strategy is how to relate G-12 groups with cell groups. I have come across so much confusion in this area that I feel the need to deal with it from the very beginning of this implementation guide.

G-12 GROUPS ARE NOT CELL GROUPS

There is a major difference between a G-12 group and an evangelizing cell group. The G-12 group meets at a particular time (often before a planned congregational or celebration service in the church building) and involves cell group leaders. Its purpose is discipleship and coaching.

Regular Open Cell	Closed G-12 Group
• Meets Weekly. • Meets Outside the Church Building. • Focuses on Evangelism. • Anyone Can Attend.	• Meets Biweekly (at ICM it meets weekly.) • Meets Inside the Church Building or a Home. • Focuses on Discipleship. • Only Cell Leaders Can Attend.

The G-12 group reaches within; the cell group reaches out. The G-12 group is for discipleship. Its purpose is to care for the cell leaders. A regular cell group evangelizes, supports, and cares for each believer. This is the principle practiced by ICM and all other effective G-12 cell churches. They do not confuse G-12 groups with cell groups.

Not everyone has the privilege of joining a G-12 group. To get into a G-12 group, you must be a cell leader. In other words, G-12 groups are groups of leaders. I remember saying this at a seminar in Philadelphia. One participant exclaimed, "So G-12 groups are groups of cell leaders. That makes sense. That's the first time I've heard it stated so plainly."[1]

Remember that a cell group is open, evangelistic, and seeks to multiply. Each cell group should possess the following characteristics:

- Meets weekly.
- Penetrates the community by meeting outside the church building.
- Focuses on evangelism.
- Provides edification for its members.
- Multiplies continually (at least once per year).

In all the worldwide cell churches I studied, the cell could be defined as *a group of 4-15 people that meets weekly outside the church building for the purpose of evangelism and discipleship with the goal of multiplication.*

I have discovered that cell churches all around the world follow a very similar definition of a cell group. You will notice incredible flexibility in the above definition. It does *not* say:

- That you have to meet in a home (many cells meet at work, the university campus, a coffee shop, etc.)

- That you have to follow the Sunday sermon (most do, but some do not.)
- That you have to have family cells (many cell groups are homogeneous men's cells, women's cells, or children's cells.)
- That you have to follow one particular cell order (e.g., the 4Ws–Welcome, Worship, Word, and Works.)
- That you have to have a certain level of participation.

I have worked with cell churches for quite some time now. In fact, cell churches have been the focus of my full-time work and study for the past eleven years. One thing I have discovered is that the most important part of the cell church is the cell group and the people in it. How we define the cell and what we expect from the cell underpins all other cell church components.

G-12 Groups Are Teams of Cell Leaders

One pastor I worked with had trouble understanding that G-12 groups are teams of cell group leaders. Since his church had not yet transitioned to cell ministry, he planned to ask his staff to find their twelve from within their particular ministries. The Christian Education person, for example, was supposed to find her G-12 group among the Sunday school teachers. Before fully implementing his plan, he asked me for counsel. I explained to him that a G-12 group was a *team of cell leaders*. His staff would continue to have their particular ministries under them, but they would also begin forming their G-12 groups from emerging cell leaders. Cell group leadership, as opposed to involvement in a ministry, is what qualifies a person to participate in a G-12 group.

As we talked, he began to see that the G-12 strategy was a way to multiply and care for cell group leaders who in turn multiplied and cared for more cell group leaders. During the next staff meeting, he explained the transition process and resulting vision to his department pastors. He shared that each of them would begin by leading a cell group, multiplying it, and eventually forming a network of cell leaders—instead of trying to find their G-12 groups among ministry leaders. This was not easy for his staff to grasp, but he clarified that there would be a transition process and that he would lead the first pilot cell group with them.

He made it clear that each pastor would continue to oversee his or her particular ministry responsibility in the church. He assured them that together they would reduce one another's ministry loads, enabling them to focus more on relationally-based cell groups, rather than task oriented activities. In the future, each staff member would be identified as a 'cell ministry pastor' as opposed to a particular 'ministry leader.'

Two Distinct Meetings

In my previous G-12 book, I wrote about Pastor Mike Osborn, the youth pastor at Harvest Assembly in Virginia Beach, Virginia. This church, unlike many North American cell churches adopting the G-12 strategy, has followed the G-12 model in its entirety. Pastor Osborn interacts regularly with Pastor Castellanos. Pastor Osborn wrote,

> The Cell is open and evangelistic. It can have any number of people in it, and it should always be growing and multiplying. The cell is an hour long and geared toward bringing new people to Christ. The G-12 meeting is closed and new people do not join it, unless they are becoming a part of your 12. This group becomes your life long group. It never multiplies, and they become your friends, and associates in the ministry.

I meet with my 12 every week, but I also lead an evangelistic cell. None of my 12 are in my cell. They all lead their own, and most of them have begun their own G-12 group in addition to their evangelistic cell.[2]

As I have interacted with churches around the world about the G-12 question, I have discovered those who struggle with understanding G-12 do so because they are not sure if the open cell group is the G-12 group and vice-versa.

David Jaramillo, pastor of The Light Church, converted a nineteen-year old stagnated program-based church into the fastest growing cell church in Ecuador. He says, "I believe it's much better to follow what they do at ICM in Bogota, which is to have two meetings completely separate." He goes on to say why:

1. "Separating the two avoids confusion. By combining the two, people don't know what a G-12 is or who belongs to it. To combine the G-12 with the open cell group confuses people.
2. "The purposes of both meetings are totally different. The G-12 meeting is to care, feed, form, and supervise leaders. The open cell group is to plant the seed and harvest the fruit.
3. "The spiritual level and participant needs are totally different in both groups. The leaders in the G-12 group have such different needs from those in the open cell group. It's impossible to fulfill the expectations of both groups if you combine the two meetings."[3]

Bethany World Prayer Center in Baker, Louisiana has adapted the ICM model by asking the daughter cell leaders to return to the mother cell group each week for the G-12 meeting. At ICM, on the other hand, these two meetings are completely separate.

At Bethany, the G-12 meeting became the same as the normal cell group. Thus, the open cell group was both an open evangelizing cell and a closed G-12 group. As soon as there is a daughter cell leader, the open cell becomes both G-12 group and open cell group rolled into one.

Is there anything wrong with new cell group leaders returning to the mother cell? Of course not. Many do this to find support and help. I would, however, avoid calling this the G-12 meeting or team gathering. Call it what it is instead: asking the daughter cell group leader to come back to the mother cell group for fellowship and encouragement. I think it is a good idea for new leaders to do this for the first couple of weeks or months.

It is also important to remember that the purpose of an open, evangelistic cell is totally different from a closed, discipleship and supervision group for leaders. What the new leader truly needs is coaching, mentoring, and discipleship—not an open cell meeting!

Bethany World Prayer Center has recently changed their approach and now comes closer to reflecting the two meeting approach. Larry Stockstill wrote: "We now have the cell leaders meet as an open cell until they have three leaders under them. Then, they can start their 'twelve' meeting. It usually meets right after the open cell as a closed cell. Our open cells only last for one hour so it is pretty easy for the second meeting to take place (it can happen before as well). This prevents the meeting happening at a 'second time.'"[4]

I am grateful to Bethany for their work in adapting the G-12 strategy. Throughout this book, I want to demonstrate the importance of following principles rather than models. Bethany has pioneered the cell church path for many U.S. cell churches, and I respect them greatly.

A GREAT ADAPTED G-12 EXAMPLE

The Liverpool Christian Life Centre (LCLC) near Sydney, Australia only recently transitioned to the cell church strategy and already has over 125 cell groups and 2500 attending celebration services. Senior Pastor John McMartin and Pastor Andrew Harper have done an excellent job in forming their G-12 system. I would like to say that I created the G-12 structure at Liverpool Christian Life Centre, but in reality, I simply observed what they were already doing and liked it so much I want to recommend it to you.

At LCLC, cell groups meet weekly outside the church building for the purpose of evangelizing, discipling, and multiplying. All staff and lay G-12 leaders facilitate an open cell group during the week—even the senior pastor. The message rings loud and clear: as a cell church, all members are battling to reach lost people through cell groups.

LCLC clearly distinguishes between closed G-12 groups and open, evangelizing cells. The open cell group at LCLC penetrates the community, reaches lost people, and simultaneously disciples the newer believers. The G-12 group, on the other hand, is for cell group leaders to receive ongoing coaching and care.

The G-12 groups meet biweekly (every other week) on Sunday night in the church building before the normal evening service (Sunday evening services are still common in Australia.) Since the G-12 meeting is biweekly, on one week a cell leader meets with his parent G-12 leader (the leader from whose group he multiplied) and the next week the cell leader meets with the G-12 group he has established/is establishing (those leaders who have multiplied from his group.)

If the cell leader has multiplied only one time, it will be a one-on-one meeting. As soon as he multiplies again, it will be a one-on-two meeting, etc. The number in each G-12 group depends on how many times the cell leader has multiplied his or her cell. While one G-12 group meeting might have twelve, another might have only three or four.[5]

The message that Pastor McMartin gives to his own G-12 group is transcribed and distributed to all of the G-12 leaders to use in their G-12 groups (in the same way that the pastor's sermon is used in the open cell groups.) Pastor Harper writes, "The material that we teach in the G-12s that comes from our parent G-12 is leadership material and is at a different level when compared to what is taught in the cells. Our leaders have different challenges and need to be challenged differently."[6]

All of these G-12 groups meet for one hour before the Sunday evening service in part because it saves time. This is beneficial for two reasons:

- It does not require 'another night out.'
- It assures that the G-12 meeting will take place.

I have found that when we ask G-12 leaders to meet *anytime*, they often fail to find the time and thus fail to meet. Flexibility is great, but it does have its limits. (Note that the G-12 group could also take place in a home. The most important point is that the meetings do take place and that coaching actually happens.)

Is the G-12 system at Liverpool Christian Life Centre perfect? No. Does it practically and creatively demonstrate what a G-12 group is all about? Yes. Are there other ways to run the team gatherings? Certainly. LCLC is an important example because:

- It asks all leaders to lead open cell groups.
- LCLC does not label its cell groups as G-12 groups.
- LCLC ministers to the leaders in distinct gatherings and to cell members in other gatherings.

Can daughter cell leaders continue to return to the mother cell group for additional support and fellowship at LCLC? Of course, with the understanding that the true G-12 meeting takes place on Sunday night.

Closed G-12 groups coach cell leaders. Open cell groups evangelize non-Christians and edify believers. G-12 groups can meet in the church building and do not have to meet weekly. Open cell groups should meet weekly outside the building, to provide a foundation for the church which gathers together in celebration. Understanding and applying the differences between the two types of groups will help you to stay on track and more effectively minister to your target audience.

3

FROM TWELVE
TO THREE

The number twelve has great significance in the Word of God. Jacob had twelve sons and there were twelve tribes of Israel. Jesus chose twelve disciples, and in Acts 2 the disciples felt it necessary to replace Judas Iscariot to bring the number back to twelve. The Hebrew year was divided into twelve months and the day into twelve hours. The number twelve is linked with the elective purposes of God.[1]

For the International Charismatic Mission, the number twelve has special significance for their G-12 vision. If you were to visit them, you would see banners hanging from the ceiling, proclaiming the number twelve. Everyone is looking for their twelve disciples. Pastor Castellanos testifies that the vision of the government of twelve disciples was given to him by the Lord as a direct revelation for ICM. Therefore the number twelve is very significant to them. There is an excitement in the air and it is working for them.

Not every church will be called to focus on the number twelve like ICM is. Therefore, we must wrestle with the significance of this number to try to seek the principle that underlies the practice of gathering twelve disciples.

The number twelve is not the only number that carries great weight in the Bible. There were *three* disciples who had special intimacy with Jesus, Jesus was raised up on the *third* day, and there were *three* crosses at Calvary. God created the heavens and earth in *seven* days, the sabbatical year occurred every *seven* years. The day of Atonement occurred in the *seventh* month. *Seven* signified fulfillment and perfection. The number *ten* signifies completeness, as illustrated in the Ten Commandments. *Forty* is associated with God's mighty acts in the history of Israel and the church.

On top of this, the New Testament provides no evidence that the apostles or other church leaders attached any significance to a specific number of disciples chosen in a church. In Acts, the New Testament history book, you will not find the apostles diligently looking for twelve disciples in order to follow Jesus' pattern of twelve disciples. In order to apply theological significance to a particular number of disciples in the church today, it is necessary for the entire Bible to give witness to this practice. I find no substantiation for the idealization of the number twelve or any other number in Acts or the Epistles. In addition, it is absent in the rest of church history and 2,000 years of theological development.

ICM has heard God's call for every member in their church to develop twelve disciples. They are using this strategy to become one of the largest churches in the history of the church. Some churches will feel called to follow ICM's strategy and focus on the number twelve. Others will choose to base their strategy on the principles that lie behind the number.

From Idealism to Reality

During one particular week-long seminar, a participant came up to me after my G-12 lesson saying,

> Joel, could you please explain this G-12 thing in a more practical way? I have many fellow pastors with me who are hungry for cell ministry. I know from experience that if they think you're theorizing, they will most likely reject the whole thing. Please clarify.

God spoke to me through that pastor. I knew that I had to change my G-12 lesson and give it an injection of practicality. I continued pondering G-12 practicality on the long drive home. I had invited Porfirio Ludeña, co-founder and senior pastor of the Republic Church, to join me. As we traveled together in my car, we talked earnestly and sincerely about our own experiment with the G-12 strategy. We were enthralled by the 'possibilities' of growth through twelve, but our reality was so much different. At that time, we had close to 250 cells and six people on staff, but we were not coaching our new leaders effectively. We were depending too heavily on the staff pastors to motivate the troops.

Most of our staff had visited ICM more than once, and we had even hosted a G-12 seminar in our church by one of Pastor Castellanos' twelve disciples. Our problem was not a failure to understand the G-12 strategy; it was asking busy lay people to lead a cell, multiply it twelve times, and then care for each new leader. Our middle-class church leaders were simply not buying it. Instead of motivating, we noticed that the lay congregation slid into glazed stares.

That day, we finally admitted to each other that our infrastructure was not healthy. "Do you really think a lay person can multiply his or her cell twelve times and then care for those twelve leaders?" I asked him. "In our congregation," he replied, "it would truly be a miracle."

We came to the point of acknowledging that the number twelve for busy lay people in our setting was too high. It was not based on reality—for us. It did not motivate people to action. We reflected on our visits to the Elim cell church in San Salvador and how their coaches supervised up to five cell leaders. Although our coaching system highlighted multiplication without division, their coaching actually worked better—even though we were glorying in using G-12 principles.

As we talked, we discovered two crucial points:

1. Most of our cell leaders would be able to envision multiplying their cells three to five times. We agreed that a lay leader would be able to oversee three groups that were birthed out of his or her group.

2. A cell overseer or cell coach would be more effective when he or she continued leading a cell group. We noticed that some cell churches ask their supervisors to stop leading open cell groups when they begin coaching other cell leaders. Such supervisors become experts in telling other people what to do, while they themselves are neither winning people to Jesus nor exercising their spiritual muscles in the open cell atmosphere. We found that when upper leaders are only supervising and not in the battle of touching people in an open cell, hierarchical stagnation occurred. "Leading an open cell and caring for three daughter cell leaders would be manageable," we concluded.

God was present in our conversation that day as we worked through our ministry troubles and developed a new method. As James said, "It seemed good to the Holy Spirit and to us" (Acts 15:28).

Introducing the G-12.3 Structure

After working through the problems we faced and combining the two foundational principles we discovered, I developed the G-12.3 concept. G-12.3 is not a fixed model that needs to be followed in a rigid, non-flexible manner. It is built upon principles which are adaptable to different situations.

In the G-12.3 structure, a full-time pastor oversees twelve cell leaders, while a lay leader envisions caring for three daughter cell leaders and continues to lead an open cell group. The number three is a more realistic and manageable number that gives lay volunteers a feasible goal: multiply the original cell three times and care for each one of those leaders while continuing to lead the original cell.

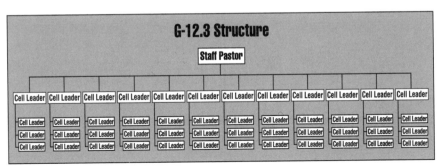

Fig. 1: The G-12.3 Structure

The G-12.3 continues to use all of the principles from the G-12 model (i.e., multiplication without division, every member a cell leader, every leader a supervisor, etc.) It simply reduces the load on lay leaders to three.

Several churches have come to the similar conclusions independently of ours at the Republic Church. David Brandon, pastor of Newmarket Alliance Church in Ontario, Canada, said, "As far as the application of G-12 has gone—we have adjusted our approach to what we would call G-3."[2] Steven L. Ogne, church planter and coaching consultant, says,

> Most of the ideal systems you see described in small group seminars these days say the ratio should be one to five or even one to ten. I'll tell you what, in my experience in our busy society, coaches are much more effective when they are coaching one to three group leaders. It really does allow them to visit the groups. It really does allow them to have enough time to build relationship, and it reduces the stress on them...Go for the connections that work, not the pretty organizational chart.[3]

In this structure, a staff pastor would lead a G-12 (Group A below.) Each G-12 members would lead a weekly open cell group (Group C) and a G-3 group (Group B.) The members of the G-3 would lead weekly open cell groups (Groups D.)

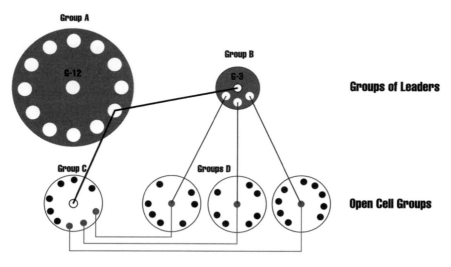

Fig. 2: G-12.3 Graphic View

The grey lines at the bottom of the diagram illustrate how the G-3 members move from being cell group members to cell group leaders. Once a cell member begins to lead a group (Group D), he or she need not continue to attend the first group (Group C.)

Is Three a Sacred Number?

Although the number three is important in the Bible, gathering three cell leaders into a G-3 does not unlock the door to special blessing. Pastors might, in fact, decide to ask lay leaders to care for five cell leaders. Or they might feel led to develop a G-10.5 system (staff pastors care for ten cell leaders while lay leaders care for five multiplication leaders.) The G-12.3 structure is principle-based, built upon observations of a realistic span of care between lay leaders and multiplication leaders.

At the Republic Church, we chose three because it was a feasible number of groups for a volunteer leader to oversee. We discovered that lay people could immediately get their hands on it. We also discovered that lay people in training to become cell leaders can grasp the vision of multiplying a cell three times and caring for those three leaders much better than multiplying a cell twelve times.

Can the Group Go Beyond Three?

What if a lay person wants to care for more than three? My response to this question is, "What a blessed problem!" If a lay leader wants to continue to lead his own cell and continue multiplying leaders beyond three, encourage him to, "Go for it!" If a lay leader says, "I have already multiplied my cell three times and am caring for those leaders, but I plan on multiplying my cell again and want to supervise him too," encourage him.

Starting with a goal of three enables lay leaders to grasp the vision with firm purpose, without feeling overwhelmed. They can expand beyond three because they are in a leadership cell above them that provides guidance and support when they need it.

The number three simply reduces the coaching goal to reasonable proportions. It is not intended to be a legalistic straightjacket on a fruitful cell leader. On the contrary, it is intended to give practical hope that it is perhaps possible to fulfill the goal of multiplying three times and someday even surpass that.

HELP THE THREE FIND THEIR OWN THREE

True success occurs when a mother cell leader has multiplied three times, is leading his or her own cell group, and is helping the daughter cell leaders find their daughter cell groups. Paul said to his spiritual son Timothy, "You then, my son, be strong in the grace that is in Christ Jesus. And the things you have heard me say in the presence of many witnesses entrust to reliable men who will also be qualified to teach others" (2 Timothy 2:1-2). The person who is leading a cell group, caring for the daughter cell leaders, and also helping the daughter cell leaders multiply their own groups has truly entered fully into this vision.

The goal, therefore, of a G-12.3 leader is to help his disciples find their disciples while leading a healthy open cell group too. An effective G-12.3 leader will not be satisfied until those in her immediate group have spotted, developed, and released their own disciples.

WHO CARES FOR THE FOURTH CELL LEADER?

By fourth cell leader, I mean a cell leader developed by a mother cell after that cell leader has formed his G-12.3. The fourth cell leader should be cared for by one of the parent cell leader's three disciples (daughter cell leaders.) In other words, the fourth daughter cell leader would continue to stay in the family, but would not be cared for directly by the parent cell leader. This would put the fourth cell leader in the position of a granddaughter to the parent cell leader.

This is the result of a trade-off between the ideal (the mother directly caring for the daughter) and the practical (the mother does not have the time or energy.) However, everyone belonging to the mother cell leader's network would come together periodically for summit meetings and the mother cell leader will continue to care for the one who is caring for the grandchild.

Four to five years down the road, if everyone has multiplied their cells yearly, it may be necessary to reevaluate who supervises the original mother's new groups. Maybe at that time, the original mother cell leader might be mature enough to extend her own network to G-4, G-5, or even G-12! Better yet, this is the time to think seriously about asking this fruitful multiplication leader to join the full-time staff.

HOW LARGE CAN A NETWORK BECOME UNDER ONE PASTOR?

We know that in the G-12 care structure (or an adaptation of it), degeneration occurs at lower levels. The farther away a disciple is from the original discipler, the higher the degree of degeneration. The original twelve understand the vision. As the number of leaders between the original discipler and the new disciples grows, the more the purity and intensity of the vision fades.

Experience has shown that a network of cells begins to decline in quality once it exceeds seventy-five cell groups (remember that each full-time pastor ultimately has twelve leaders under his care, as opposed to three.) This number comes from practical, common sense experience, as opposed to hard scientific data. Billy Hornsby, former staff pastor at Bethany World Prayer Center, suggests a lower number:

> In our own experience at Bethany, we first committed to add zone pastors as the number of cell groups grew at a 25/1 ratio. We have since discovered that with the principle of twelve, that ratio can be as much as one pastor for 50 cell groups or even more. You will know when it is necessary to add pastoral staff by the workload on the existing staff. The senior pastor should develop his 'twelve' and only add staff as he needs to.[4]

Degeneration typically arises not by someone leaving his post, but rather by offering lower-quality care due to an overburdened load. In such cases, the senior pastor must step in to assure continued quality or risk future failure at the lower cell levels because pastors cannot continue providing care to so many cell leaders.

WHO WILL LEAD THE NEW NETWORK?

By now, you have probably noticed that I believe in maintaining relationships between mother cell leader and daughter cell leader. This is one of the core values behind the G-12.3 care system.

When one network under one pastor grows too large, intimate care and discipleship will suffer. I believe, therefore, that when one network reaches around seventy-five cells, it is time to multiply it.

Where will you find the new pastor to care for half of the network? I would recommend choosing a qualified, successful cell leader from within the network. Raise that person up to a full-time staff position. Doing so will maintain relationships, continuity, and authority. It is also a testimony to everyone else that higher-level leadership is an attainable goal.

INSTILLING THE VISION OF THREE EARLY

One of the most exciting churches I have worked with thus far is a church called The Light Church in Quito, Ecuador. The senior pastor, David Jaramillo, has a clear cell vision and knows how to raise up leaders. What I like about Pastor Jaramillo is the way he is able to grasp the different aspects of the cell vision without losing his focus.

Pastor Jaramillo became convinced of the G-12.3 strategy and actively promoted it, but then he went one step beyond. Pastor Jaramillo decided to instill the vision of leading a cell and multiplying it three times in the Encounter Retreat (a two-day spiritual retreat that is part of the equipping track and gives new believers victory from past bondages.)

Even the new believers in the Encounter Retreat would hear the goal of raising up three leaders. "God is going to free you and bless you. He wants to use you mightily. After you pass through the training track which will take about nine months, you'll begin to lead your own cell group. But that isn't everything. You'll also go on to multiply your cell group at least three times and you'll care for those three new leaders! You'll not only lead a cell group, but you'll also be a coach of future cell leaders."

At the Republic Church, we also began to instill in the new cell leaders the hope of one day leading a cell group and multiplying it. In fact, the vision-casting time was the culmination of the Encounter Retreat. Each new believer left the retreat with the vision of multiplication.

The number three is feasible. It is too easy to talk about 'the twelve' when the majority of the people have not even considered 'the one'—leading a cell group. It is saddening to hear example after example of cell leaders who started their G-12 treks only to stagnate along the way. Do not let this happen to you. In fact, determine that it will not happen. Start by setting feasible and realistic goals for your church members and the new believers they will reach through the dynamic power of the cell church!

4

G-12

FROM THE TOP

Peering down from the top of each church looks different for each pastor. For Pastor César Castellanos at ICM and Pastor Yonggi Cho at YFGC, the top is as high as Mount Everest. For most pastors, however, the church mountain is much smaller. But no matter how large the church, it is the senior pastor who must lead the cell vision and a G-12 team.

This does not mean that the senior pastor will immediately have twelve individuals or couples on his team. What it does mean is that the G-12 vision must flow from the top down.

A senior pastor must not delegate the cell church vision, nor the corresponding G-12 care system. Pastor Cho, the senior pastor of the largest church in the history of Christianity, says, "The [senior] pastor must be the key person involved. Without the pastor, the system will not hold together. It is a system, and a system must have a control point. The controlling factor in home cell groups is the pastor."[1] In most growing cell churches around the world, the senior pastor is the 'cell minister' in the cell church. He is the one who sets the direction and leads the charge. He must also give direction to the G-12 vision.

THE SENIOR PASTOR'S G-12 LEADERSHIP TEAM

Gather a G-12 Group

If there are several pastors already on staff, the senior pastor should pick his staff members as part of his G-12. Regardless of whether the cell church transition is just beginning or a cell care structure already exists, the senior pastor should oversee his top cell pastors. The senior pastor cannot say, "I think I'll pick Pastor Rick as one of my 12 but not Pastor Bob." Imagine the division this could cause!

If the senior pastor is just starting a pilot cell group (which means he is just beginning the cell church transition), he should pick key people he could envision discipling in the future. When the pilot cell group multiplies and each member has his or her own cell group, then the senior pastor can meet with those same cell leaders in a G-12 group. However, every member in the G-12 group must *at least* be leading a cell group. In the future, all G-12 leaders should have also multiplied their cell groups.

If the church already has cell groups but it has not yet transitioned to the G-12 care structure, the senior pastor—after much prayer and consultation with the leadership team—should pick key cell leaders to form part of an initial G-12 group. The criteria are simple: fruit and holiness. Each person on the senior pastor's G-12 team should believe in the cell church vision to the point of leading and multiplying a cell.

As I have mentioned before, a church just beginning the transition to cells or planting a cell church from scratch can expect fruitfulness to simply mean *leading a cell group*. A senior pastor whose church already has cell groups can choose for an original G-12 those people who have been the most fruitful in cell multiplication and leadership development. Of course, holiness, character, and faithfulness also play an essential role.

Focus on the G-12 Group

When there is only one pastor on staff, the most fruitful cell leaders become the leadership team (G-12 group.) In this situation, the pastor most likely will not have twelve immediately (perhaps only two, four, or six.) Ideally, the senior pastor would meet with this group of leaders on a weekly basis to entrench cell church and G-12 principles, but reality sometimes dictates a meeting every other week.

FROM PROGRAMS TO PEOPLE

In today's fast-paced church where so many demands are placed on a pastor, it is easy to focus on running the church rather than discipling key leaders. Just to make it to the end of the week with a sigh of relief is a challenge for many pastors. The program has become so heavy, the schedule so tight. Because there is no one else to oversee the building project, set up childcare for the Saturday rally, or hone the Sunday service, the pastor ends up taking charge of everything.

Some pastors operate as if their primary job is to be involved with everything. They focus on perfecting the Sunday program and keeping the church administration running smoothly throughout the week to the detriment of their cell leaders. Many pastors spend their time and energy on programs rather than people.

For the G-12 system to work, the philosophy of the senior pastor must change. The senior pastor must ease off on managing programs and spend more time discipling people—especially his key G-12 people. He must change from running the church machine to mentoring key leaders who will disciple leaders who will disciple even more leaders.

PASTORAL CARE

The senior pastor must pour his life into his key leaders. He must build relationships with them outside of the official team gathering. Jesus, the ultimate G-12 leader, revealed how He developed relationships with His disciples: "I no longer call you servants, because a servant does not know his master's business. Instead, I have called you *friends*, for everything that I learned from my Father I have made known to you" (John 15:15).

Jesus did not simply teach His disciples about prayer. He asked them to accompany Him to prayer meetings. He allowed His disciples to see Him praying. When the disciples finally asked Him what He was doing, He seized the opportunity to teach them about prayer (Luke 11:1-4). The same is true with evangelism. Jesus evangelized people in the presence of His disciples and then instructed them afterwards. He took advantage of real life situations to explain complex doctrinal issues (e.g., the rich young ruler in Matthew 19:23).

The best pastors usually befriend their key leaders and minister into their lives. One successful pastor in Australia explained why his G-12 network was growing so rapidly by saying, "I'm a friend to my leaders. Those under me follow my example and they befriend the new small group leaders under their care. Through friendship, my network of cell leaders has grown larger than any other."

The gospel writer Mark describes the calling of the twelve this way: "He appointed twelve—designating them apostles—that they might be with him…" (Mark 3:14). Jesus prioritized "being with them" over a set of rules or techniques.

Many G-12 members are looking for their senior pastor to lead them but also to "be with them." One staff pastor said to me, "My senior pastor never spends time with me. He administrates me, directs me, and even exemplifies how to lead a cell group by doing it. But what I really want is a friend. I want someone to take me out for coffee, to occasionally 'hang out with.'"

There are many practical ways to befriend key G-12 leaders. Here are a few suggestions:

- Invite a G-12 leader (and spouse or family) to your home for dinner. Let them see your family, your dog, your life.
- Go out for coffee with a G-12 leader.
- Invite a cell group leader to play sports with you, or some other normal life activity.
- Pray daily for your G-12 leaders (this will solidify your spiritual friendship.)
- Send a G-12 leader a birthday card, a Get Well note, or a spontaneous, 'off the wall' humorous letter.
- Minister to a particular need in his or her life.

PREPARE FOR THE G-12 MEETING

If your church is blessed enough to have a full-time staff, make them part of the leadership team (G-12 group). When you have a regular G-12 group gathering, the first order of business is to minister to your leaders through the Word and prayer. The goal of this meeting time is to edify them and minister to their needs, while expecting your team to be accountable for those leaders under their care.

The teaching you give to them can then be distributed to each G-12 leader to use in his or her team gathering, and thus your message and God-given burden will spread throughout the entire leadership structure.

After ministering to your leaders, ask each of them to report on his or her cell network. It is best if everyone has as a complete set of statistics for each network represented in the team gathering (I will explain more about networks in a later chapter.) Statistical reporting is an important tool for maintaining the health of each cell network. Reports for each cell network should include multiplication goals, groups that met the previous week, the number of people attending cells, potential leaders in training, etc.

Since each pastor (or lay leader) will have a written copy of the report, everyone can follow along while each pastor talks. Each pastor is free to ask questions like, "John, I noticed that Mary's cell group hasn't met in awhile, is she still leading the group?" Godly accountability will help keep everyone on track.

STAY INVOLVED IN MINISTRY

Apart from caring for a G-12 group, I encourage senior pastors (as well as all staff pastors) to lead an open cell group. The most important reason for a senior pastor to lead his own cell group is to stay close to the fire and maintain practical experience in winning others to Jesus. This also prevents the senior pastor from losing touch with cell group leaders joining the battle on a daily basis.

When his cell group multiplies, I encourage the senior pastor to give the daughter cell leader to one of his G-12 leaders, rather than trying to start a separate network apart from his G-12 network. The G-12 leaders must be the senior pastor's priority. Often, when a senior pastor starts two networks, his G-12 leaders feel slighted and in the end everyone receives less of his time and ministry.

There are many arguments that would seemingly contradict a senior pastor leading an open cell group. "After all," someone might say, "shouldn't the senior pastor delegate as much as possible? Shouldn't he rotate among various groups instead of concentrating on one?" Such an argument has its merits, but in my opinion, it falls short. The benefits of leading a cell group far outweigh the shortcomings.

In each case where the senior pastor was far removed from personal involvement in cell ministry, I have witnessed a growing apathy about the cell groups. In the process of growth, the senior pastor removed himself from the life of the cell, and over time, the cell groups began to operate like a giant machine—and without proper lubrication.

Dale Galloway, the former pastor of New Hope Community Church, told me that every pastor and staff person led a cell group— even when the church had 6,000 members and 600 cell groups. He insisted that it is foolish to expect others to follow what the senior pastor fails to model.[2]

Notice the benefits of leading a cell:

- A deeper cell church vision.
- Pastoral burden for cell leaders.
- Personal interaction with non-Christians.
- Illustrations for teaching material gleaned from experience.
- Insight into which cell lessons work and which ones do not.

Above all, it declares in numerous ways that cell ministry is so important that even the senior pastor is willing to lead an evangelistic cell group.

I once consulted with a 3,500-member church that was transitioning to the cell church model. When I talked about the importance of the senior pastor leading a cell group, the senior pastor immediately responded to my counsel. For too long, he had felt the inadequacy of announcing on Sunday morning that everyone needed to participate in cell ministry when he was not even involved. He and his wife began leading a professional couples group and have multiplied it two times.

The long-term success of cell ministry depends on adjusting cell church principles to each church's reality. The best laboratory is personal involvement. When a pastor leads a cell group, he captures the weekly benefits of cell ministry and can relate to fellow cell leaders in the church. As Clarence Day once said, "Information's pretty thin stuff, unless mixed with experience."[3]

Leading a cell group, as opposed to attending a cell group, allows the senior pastor to experience the need to invite non-Christians, train new leaders, prepare the study time, and shepherd those in need. It also gives the pastor the chance to determine if his own cell lesson (based on his Sunday morning message) edifies the saints and speaks to non-Christians.

Granted, there might be periods of time when the senior pastor no longer leads an open cell group. Many senior pastors of the world's largest cell churches do not personally lead a cell group. These churches have reached another level: most likely, the senior pastor already has an intense passion for cell ministry and thus might not need to lead a cell to keep him connected. The norm always has its exceptions and there are probably times when this rule can be broken safely. But initially, and for quite some time into the cell church experience, the senior pastor should be leading a group of his own.

ADDING STAFF BASED ON PAST SUCCESS

If you are thinking of adding staff to your church, do so on the basis of past success in cell multiplication. You do not have to be as radical as the International Charismatic Mission. ICM considers a person *part-time* staff when the person has developed a network of 250 cell groups. A full-time staff member must have multiplied his or her network to 500 cell groups. In your situation, you might require a person to have developed a network of 5-10 cell groups to be considered as a potential staff member. Just make sure that the person has demonstrated past success in cell multiplication.

All of the largest cell churches in the world operate this way. They will not elevate anyone into a higher position unless the person has demonstrated success at the lower levels. Calling and personal qualities are essential, but the ultimate test is past success as a cell leader, cell supervisor, etc. For the most part, seminary training is not a major factor in elevation to top leadership.

It is usually best to raise up staff members from within the church. This was the pattern in the leading cell churches worldwide. These churches did not have to look beyond themselves to fill their top leadership positions. All leadership had to go through the normal channels of ministerial experience, ministerial success, and leadership training within the church before being lifted up to higher positions.

From their extensive studies of successful businesses, C. Collins and Jerry I. Porras concluded, "The visionary companies were six times more likely to promote insiders. Of the 113 CEOs in the visionary companies, only 3.5 % came from outside."[4] It makes sense; those who have risen from within intimately understand and will operate with the vision and philosophy of the company, or in our case, the church.

THE MAIN TASK OF THE LEADERSHIP TEAM: LEADERSHIP DEVELOPMENT

Carl George says, "The role of the church staff is to effectively manage the leadership development structures."[5] The main role of pastors is not to manage church programs but to develop, manage, and care for cell group leaders. As each pastor cares for his G-12, he will in turn care for each member's network of leaders and the process will continue throughout the church.

I consulted with one church whose staff focused week after week on the Sunday service. The goal of the staff meeting was to prepare for Sunday morning. It was a clear case of a pastoral staff existing for the Sunday celebration.

I spent the weekend with the staff, encouraging each one of them to oversee a network of cell groups (at that time they were not even meeting as a G-12 group). I counseled them to start the pastoral meeting by examining each network of cells and only afterwards to focus on the celebration service. The senior pastor and pastoral team were willing to adjust and prioritize cell group leadership development and care as the main task of the church. The senior pastor later wrote to me,

> ...our staff is totally on board and committed to the [cell church] philosophy and a large part is because they are seeing the results in people's lives. They also like the fact that they have a very specific ministry approach to follow and directions on how to make it happen: i.e. get people through the training, work with leaders, get apprentices, etc. It is less nebulous than a generic 'get people to come to your events'—or 'build a ministry'—it is training lay people for a very specific role and directions—and they have a plan on how to do it.

The reason for having pastors on staff in the cell church is to produce new leaders to reap the harvest. Paul tells us in Ephesians 4:11-12, "It was he who gave some to be apostles, some to be prophets, some to be evangelists, and some to be pastors and teachers, to prepare God's people for works of service, so that the body of Christ may be built up." Make sure that full-time staff is doing what these passages clearly prescribe: preparing the saints for works of service.

EACH PASTOR OVER A MINISTRY

As stated, each staff person should primarily oversee a network of cells (G-12.3.) It is a good idea, however, for each staff person to also be responsible for a particular ministry.

As the church grows, you will find that there is more to cell church than cells. Take the Sunday celebration. Someone must lead worship, reach out to those who receive Jesus, train the children, count the offerings, and serve as ushers. Who will be in charge of these various ministries? I believe it is best to place a staff person over each one of these ministries (recent church plants or churches without a staff could place key cell leaders over these ministries.) I do not believe the cell church should hire pastors with a particular job area, such as Worship, Christian Education, Visitation, or any other common ministry. Each pastor's primary responsibility should be to care for a network of cell groups. Above and beyond the cell network responsibility, each staff pastor should have at least one ministry responsibility.

One of the pastors at the cell church I co-founded leads a network of homogeneous cell groups among families and young professionals. He is also in charge of follow-up with those who receive Jesus during the celebration services. Another pastor is responsible for the ministry of ushers, although he heavily delegates the major functions to others.

After we talk about the health of each cell network in the G-12 team gathering, this pastor might say, "I'm going to have a meeting for new ushers. I need the names of faithful cell leaders (or those who are in the process of becoming cell leaders) who would be interested in serving in this ministry." Then, as a pastoral team, we offer him names of potential ushers.[6]

Because we want to maintain cell ministry as the base of our church, we will not allow people in the congregation to participate in ministries unless they are faithfully attending a cell group. We would even like them to be in the training track to eventually become cell group leaders, since this should be the goal of every member. The main point is not to allow those ministries to become programs that compete with cell groups for time and resources.

G-12 ministry cannot be viewed solely from the top. Although the senior pastor must envision, implement, model, and disciple, we must consider the crucial role of lay supervisors. Next, we will look at the G-12 church from the perspective of the lay coach.

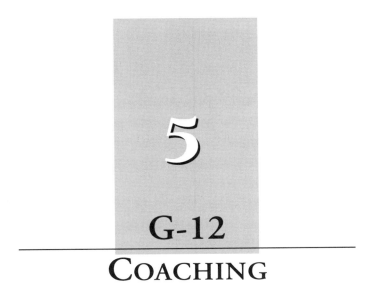

G-12

COACHING

Because the G-12 strategy is based on relationships, every G-12 leader must know how to develop relationships with the cell leaders under her care. This means that staff members will mentor lay leaders and the lay leaders will do the same with the leaders under them. The best way to describe this mentoring relationship is *coaching*.

The longer I am involved in cell church ministry, the more I realize the importance of coaching. Coaching keeps the cell structure oiled. Pastor Cho says, "The most important role in cell ministry is that of the section leader (coach.)"[1] A coach in the G-12.3 structure is a cell leader who steps to the next level of leadership and begins caring for her daughter cell leaders. As the mother cell leader coaches the new cell leader, she will feel a new confidence and commitment to press ahead.

Do Not Depend on Staff to Do All Coaching

Do not depend on the staff to coach cell leaders! The danger lies in stifling the growth by creating a care barrier. As the cell system grows, staff pastors should focus on leaders of leaders (those who have multiplied their cells), rather than on every individual cell group leader. In other words, you must come to the point of entrusting lay people to care for new cell group leaders.

Without clear, systematic teaching on how to coach, lay leaders tend to drop the ball. They do not know what to do. When that happens, the pastor must step in, which can create an unhealthy dependence upon the pastor. This happened to us at the Republic Church.

We multiplied rapidly, but we did not adequately prepare our cell leaders to coach their multiplication leaders. Because we failed to promote a clear-cut system of expecting lay people to care for their leaders, nothing happened. The responsibility fell on the pastoral team. We worked and worked and worked, yet our unwillingness to delegate assured slow growth at best. We could not grow beyond our own ability to care. The cracks of fatigue finally caught up with us and we began to produce unhealthy cell groups. From this we learned that lay people need training to learn how to care for lay cell group leaders. Our mistakes taught us to change and eventually we developed the G-12.3 coaching system.

As you read this book and grasp how to implement coaching in your church, you will avoid our mistakes and successfully prepare your G-12 leaders to coach their multiplication leaders.

Developing Coaches

The most exciting cell churches in the world today believe not only that everyone can become a cell group leader, but that everyone can become a coach as well! This is where the secret of their success lies. It is essential to prepare everyone to coach, not just lead. We need to give people a vision beyond leading one cell; we need to take them into coaching new cell group leaders.

People are longing for a vision beyond themselves. They are longing for something to sustain them for the long term. If their only goal is leading a cell group and they arrive at that place, they will likely become bored and stagnate.

It is my conviction that the best time to cast vision for coaching is before each person becomes a cell leader. When you instill a vision in a person at an early age in his Christian development, he will be prepared to follow it later. It will be necessary to revisit coaching later on, but it helps to teach coaching techniques during the initial training track (such coaching tips can be used to care for cell members or later on to coach a new cell group leader.)

Assure each leader that coaching new leaders will not happen overnight. But by setting forth the vision early on, you will create excitement and purpose right away. Make sure that some teaching on supervision is included in the training track—at least by the last manual on cell leadership. It is best to tell them this at the Encounter Retreat (explained in detail in Chapter 7.) After being set free from sin, new believers are guided to serve in a ministry that will challenge them to live in holiness and useful service.

The exciting graduation of the equipping track takes place when the member begins his or her own cell group. But it does not stop there. The new leader will multiply his or her cell and will then seek to coach three new cells![2]

KEY REASONS FOR COACHING

All successful cell churches around the world realize that long-term cell success depends on the quality of their coaching. Most of them have learned this through failure. They have multiplied coach-less groups, only to see them wither away, or worse yet, become cancerous. The following will help you to understand why coaches are so essential.[3]

Coaching allows a cell church to release cell leaders who are less than perfect.

I recently watched my fourth grade daughter play basketball. It was painful. She didn't know what to do. At times she twiddled her hands behind her back, hoping that no one would pass her the ball. She cried during and after that first game. Even so, the first game showed her how much she needed to learn.

The week following that fateful first game, my daughter soaked up knowledge like a sponge as I taught her how to rebound, steal the ball, play defense, and shoot. We practiced every day, and I did not have to convince her to practice.

On the other hand, my first grade daughter had no interest in practicing with us. She dutifully came along, but possessed no desire to play. The difference? Experience. My oldest daughter felt the need to improve. She saw her own lack after playing her first game.

Maturity does not come from sitting on the sidelines. It comes from being involved in the game and seeing the need. Coaches offer a helping hand to those wanting to play better, to lead better. Strong coaching assures that the cell leader is never left alone. The coach is constantly watching over his or her shoulder, whispering words of counsel and encouragement.

I began leading my first small group when I was three years old in the Lord. Sure, I made a lot of mistakes, but I learned from them. I grew as a result of them. When I look back at that cell experience, I see it as one of the most important in my life. It truly changed me and set my course for the rest of my life.

Your church must be prepared to view every member of the church as a potential leader. Leaders must be trained and released quickly, not put through years of mind-numbing training. I often hear objections like, "How can this be?" or "Such a leader would be so immature!" And there is some truth in such objections. But what the doubters fail to realize is that with a great system of coaching, a new leader is *never* abandoned. A new leader begins facilitating the cell by holding someone else's hand—the coach.

Coaching enables pastors to catch problems before they become major difficulties.

Medicine is for people who are sick. Preventative medicine keeps people from getting sick in the first place. Coaches focus on using the techniques of preventative medicine. Since they have experience in leading a cell group, they can warn cell leaders of potential pitfalls.

What kind of problems am I referring to? Doubt, despair, and sexual sins to name a few. Actually, any past sin can be used by the enemy to assault the new cell leader. Rather than resist, the new cell leader might decide to give way to the sin. The coach needs to approach the situation with the counsel of Paul in Galatians 6:1-5:

> Brothers, if someone is caught in a sin, you who are spiritual should restore him gently. But watch yourself, or you also may be tempted. Carry each other's burdens, and in this way you will fulfill the law of Christ. If anyone thinks he is something when he is nothing, he deceives himself. Each one should test his own actions. Then he can take pride in himself, without comparing himself to somebody else, for each one should carry his own load.

The coach knows that satan would like the cell leader to fall into a tail spin. If sinning is not enough, satan and his army of demons would like the new cell leader to feel condemned by the action, unclean, and unable to serve. Satan delights when the cell servant finally renounces all cell involvement.

Effective coaches see problems before they become problems. They are right there to guide cell leaders through the healing process, knowing that all of us at one time have fallen.

Coaching helps to guard against Absolam spirits developing power.

Absolam was King David's errant son who succeeded in winning the hearts of Israel over to himself (2 Samuel 15). Some pastors reject cell ministry altogether because they fear an Absolam might develop. In a properly administered cell church, every leader is under the watchful eye of another coach. A good coach catches the symptoms of rebellion and will point them out before they negatively affect others. In this sense the coach fulfills the role of a shepherd, watching out for those under his or her care. Paul's advice to the pastors in Ephesus is helpful to every coach:

> Keep watch over yourselves and all the flock of which the Holy Spirit has made you overseers. Be shepherds of the church of God, which he bought with his own blood. I know that after I leave, savage wolves will come in among you and will not spare the flock. Even from your own number men will arise and distort the truth in order to draw away disciples after them. So be on your guard! (Acts 20:28-31).

Good pastoral care involves rotating among the three cell groups under each coach. I would suggest that the coach visit one of the cell groups under his care each month. During that time, the coach should observe the meeting, participate in the discussion, and afterwards offer encouragement and suggestions to the cell leader. If the coach's own cell group meets on the same night as the other cell groups, this will mean that the coach occasionally allows another member to lead the cell while he visits the cell groups under his care.

Coaching helps identify interns and potential leaders.

A good coach will offer gentle reminders about cell reproduction. "George, who are you preparing to lead the next group?" or "Have you told the group about the greater purpose of cell multiplication?" Coaches are people who have successfully multiplied their own cell groups. They can spot the tendency toward stagnation, while gently encouraging the cell leader to give birth. Often a cell leader does not know what to look for in an intern or new leader. He is trying to discover talent, gifting, or personality. Perhaps the cell leader has not gotten beyond looking at physical, outward characteristics. This is where a more experienced coach provides help in discerning spiritual values. A coach provides the ability to see the larger work of God.

Helping a leader give birth is a crucial role for a coach. It involves some teaching that mostly comes from personal experience. An effective coach is one who has been there and who simply reminds the leader that everything is going to work out—that the new birth will survive and that the mother group will not die in the process.

WHAT GREAT COACHES DO

Provide prayer support.

Cell group leaders are front-line warriors, attacking the enemy in his own territory. And the devil does not allow it to happen without a fight. In fact, he levels his heavy artillery at them. Coaches protect their cell leaders by covering them with a prayer shield that can withstand even the fiercest assaults.

Prayer provides air cover for people on the front lines. It provides the shield so desperately needed to protect them from enemy attack. Paul shares a very revealing truth in 1 Corinthians 5:3: "Even though I am not physically present, I am with you in spirit. And I have already passed judgment on the one who did this, just as if I were present." The only way that Paul could actually be present was through prayer. Prayer power allows the more experienced coach to be with the new cell leader at all times—even though he or she is physically absent.

Do not cease to hold new cell leaders up in prayer. Make it a daily, continual commitment. Each cell leader needs this prayer more than you could ever know.

Provide care through friendship.

As a researcher, I have spent many hours trying to discover the principles behind effective coaching. I have searched for secret formulas and hidden mysteries. When I finally found what I consider the key, I was embarrassed by its simplicity. I felt like the famous German theologian who boiled down all his years of research into one phrase: *Jesus loves me this I know / for the Bible tells me so.*

Friendship. This is the key. Knowledge, skill training, problem solving, group dynamics, and other techniques can play an important role in a coach's success. But what a new small group leader really needs is someone to bear the burden, to share the journey, and to serve as a sounding board. Does this mean that the actual coaching meeting is unimportant? No. Does it mean that you should not faithfully rotate among groups or provide needed skill training? No. What it does mean is that you first must win the leader through a caring friendship. Everything else will flow naturally.

Everyone can be a friend, although only some coaches will excel in administration. Everyone can be a friend, although only some coaches possess speaking gifts, a graduate level education, or a call to full-time ministry.

I would like to encourage you to start building sincere, caring relationships with those whom you are coaching. As you do, you will discover how such a simple truth can have such a powerful impact on people's lives. Be assured that, as you model friendship, those who you coach will care for their members in the same way you have coached them. Like father like son. Like mother like daughter.

Huddle up with cell leaders.

I do not know when the word 'huddle' emerged in cell circles, but it is a useful term. Think of a football coach calling his players to huddle up during a time-out. The purpose is to give instructions, calm nerves, and refocus in order to play better ball.

Many cell churches ask their coaches to huddle with their leaders once per week. It is best to discern the needs of your leaders. A biweekly huddle is also effective at maintaining quality care and control. I used to advocate a monthly huddle, but I have since discovered that too much can happen in thirty days to warrant waiting that long. Satan could take advantage of troublesome situations before help could arrive.

Cell coaches huddle with their cell leaders every other week to go over strategy, recast the vision, teach valuable skills, and minister God's Word. During huddle time, the cell coach should minister to the cell leaders through the Word and prayer. The huddle is a great time to teach needed small group dynamic skills. In the G-12.3 structure, the coach might facilitate a lesson handed down from the senior pastor.

Supervise through administration.

A coach is not the senior pastor. He is a liaison between the cell group leader and higher level leadership. As a liaison, the coach must communicate with the pastor about what is happening in the cell groups.

Coaches help remind cell group leaders to submit weekly reports that list cell group attendance, conversions, prayer requests, and any other pertinent information. Cell group leaders should know before they lead their first cell groups that they will be expected to provide this regular report. Statistical reporting maintains quality control and should not be seen as a burden.

LESSONS FROM JOHN WOODEN

My dad graduated from the University of California, Los Angeles (UCLA), and school pride rubbed off on our home. Whenever UCLA played basketball, the television was turned on and all other activities ceased. This was because Coach John Wooden, the UCLA basketball coach, always managed to guide his team into the play-offs from where he often went on to win the national championship. John Wooden can teach cell coaches a few lessons:

1. Live the life you expect others to follow. Wooden never expected more from his players than he expected from himself.
2. Practice, practice, practice. Wooden trained his players until they could execute their strategy blindfolded. This is the purpose of the huddle—to review the strategy, the expectations, and the goals of cell group multiplication. The coach must provide the strategy.
3. Know the game. Wooden's coaching flowed from an expertise of basketball. Effective coaches know cell ministry. They have read

the literature and can speak from experience because they have multiplied their own cell groups.

Wooden attracted the best players because he was an excellent coach and knew how to engender respect. Wooden raised the bar, asking his players for excellence both on and off the court. He asked players to maintain good grades and high moral standards—something that he exemplified. Simply put, he held his players to their highest potential and they responded by giving him their best.

As you commit yourself to coaching those under you, let your example inspire them to expect great things from God and to attempt great things for God.

POWER PRINCIPLES
OF THE G-12 STRATEGY

6

BUILDING
PRAYER MOMENTUM

Implementing a structure based upon G-12 principles requires a high level of commitment. Not a commitment to meetings, but a deep commitment to the things of God. If your church is not committed to prayer, for example, your church will not see the fruit of G-12 or G-12.3. Some have tried to copy the G-12 structure without seeing the power principles and the structure fell flat on its face.

At the Republic Church, we thought we were prayer experts. Our pastoral team preached sermons and taught classes about the importance of prayer. We read all the material and knew the best ways to pray. However, we lacked one key ingredient: we simply were not praying.

We beat ourselves over the head time and time again. "We should be praying more. Prayer is vital to our church." Yet all of our recriminations did not change our priorities. We valued the ideal of prayer but we did not value it enough to practice it. We depended on our programs and our personal efforts to make things happen. Despite this, God, in his mercy, blessed the work of our hands.

The programs in many churches are so effective and self-sufficient that there seems to be no need for prayer. As long as the worship team performs, the pastor preaches a relevant message, and the administration flows without a hitch, everyone feels satisfied. Dependence on slick programs is a North American norm. As you examine these churches, however, you will notice a fatal flaw: the lack of transformed lives. There is no power. God almost seems to be controlled by the church's programs as well.

You can build a church without prayer and even grow numerically. But it will be a weak church that lacks power. Transfigured lives will be the exception, rather than the norm. I prefer the type of church that breathes New Testament life from every pore. The only proven way to accomplish this is through prayer. Would Jesus rebuke some of our churches today for their prayerlessness? Would He have to cast out some of the money changers who peddle programs, rather than God? Would he need to remind us, "'My house will be called a house of prayer,' but you are making it a 'den of robbers'" (Matthew 21:12)?

DEDICATE YOURSELVES TO PRAYER

Because ICM church has grown from 70 cell groups in 1991 to 20,000 cell groups today, pastors flock to that church, hoping to capture something that will make their churches grow. Pastor Castellanos says that some pastors change their name to Charismatic, hoping that the anointing of God will fall from heaven because of the name change.

Some copy the furniture or the precise administrative structure of the church. Those who try to copy the method miss the main point. The secret behind the amazing success of ICM is its commitment to prayer. God is in the midst of the amazing success there.

Only God can grant success. Cells are simply the instruments of God's mighty power. We must not trust our methodology; rather, we must trust the living God. God uses the cell church, but He refuses to be used by it. Let us remember that our God is the God of the church. We must humbly come to Him, asking Him to use us.

Paul wrote the Colossian epistle at the end of his life saying, "Devote yourselves to prayer, being watchful and thankful" (Colossians 4:2). The Greek word for *devote* literally means *to attend constantly*. To illustrate his point Paul uses the example of Epaphras, "…who is always wrestling in prayer for you, that you may stand firm in all the will of God, mature and fully assured" (Colossians 4:12). Epaphras labored fervently and constantly for the believers in Colosse. We must continually cry out, "Lord, make us like Epaphras!" Most people immediately agree that prayer is very important. But many do not understand how to create a church of prayer. Like one desperate seminar participant blurted out, "How do I make prayer the foundation of my church?" It is so much easier to talk about prayer than to pray. Allow me to offer a few suggestions.

FOLLOW THE LEADER

In 1998, the entire pastoral team of the Republic Church visited ICM. We were privileged to eat lunch with Pastor César Fajardo and his wife Claudia. During the course of our conversation, Pastor Fajardo looked straight at my senior pastor and said, "Your church will never pray beyond your example, pastor." This not only sliced into the heart of my senior pastor but deeply moved each pastor present. We left Bogota that year with a firm commitment to *dedicate ourselves to prayer*. We realized that if the generals were not praying, the army was not going to go near the battlefield. Now things have changed. We are no longer telling the troops what to do from behind comfortable desks.

We as pastors are intimately involved in the prayer life of the church. Each staff pastor leads a three-hour segment of weekly prayer in the church—including the senior pastor. Peter Wagner says it so well,

> The senior pastor must take direct charge of the corporate prayer ministry of the church. The day-to-day implementation of various aspects of the prayer ministry can be delegated to the church prayer leader and others, but if the pastor is not perceived by the congregation as the supreme leader of corporate prayer, it will not fly as it should.[1]

This does not mean the senior pastor needs to do everything related to prayer. I recently visited a dynamic, growing cell church in Wimberley, Texas called Cypress Creek Church (CCC.) Rob Campbell, the founding pastor, understood the importance of prayer from the very beginning. He not only exemplified prayer to the congregation through his personal example, but he also staffed CCC based on the importance of intercession by bringing aboard a Pastor of Prayer, Cecilia Belvin, who has a wonderful gift of intercession to lead the prayer ministry. The first recruitment call that Pastor Campbell made—even prior to the official launch of CCC—was asking Cecilia to lead CCC's prayer ministry team. Today Cypress Creek Church has one of the most vital prayer ministries I have ever seen.

PROMOTE A VARIETY OF PRAYER FORMATS

Concentrate on cell ministry. But remember, prayer is *not* another program. It is the life of the church. It is the atmosphere in which Jesus Christ lives and works. Do your best to promote prayer at every level of the church. Here are few suggestions for implementing prayer on many levels.

Twenty-four Hour Prayer Meeting

I am committed to this idea and constantly promote it. This strategy has worked so well for us, and my prayer is that it will work for you as well. I like it so much because those leading the charge are the generals—the pastors of the church. Allow me to explain. A twenty-four hour prayer meeting takes place takes place within the church one day each week (although we now have an 18 hour weekly prayer meeting because people simply did not come between 12 P.M. and 6 A.M.) Key leaders in the church take turns leading the various prayer intervals. Those who attend the church (both cell and celebration) are encouraged to attend at anytime during the prayer meeting. They might stay for fifteen minutes, half an hour, one and one half hours, or the entire three hour time block. What matters most is that the pastors are praying.

We have six pastors in our church. Each pastor leads a three-hour interval to complete the eighteen hours. Here is our example:

- 6-9 A.M.: Pastor 1 in charge
- 9-12 A.M.: Pastor 2 in charge
- 12-3 P.M.: Pastor 3 in charge
- 3-6 P.M.: Pastor 4 in charge
- 6-9 P.M.: Pastor 5 in charge
- 9-12 P.M.: Pastor 6 in charge

I am not saying that only full-time workers can lead these prayer intervals. I do think it is important, however, that key church leaders lead a prayer segment. Sheep follow the shepherd. If prayer is important in the church, the people with influence must demonstrate their commitment. Perhaps there is only one pastor in your church. If so, you could try to find key lay leaders who could fill each block. I would recommend that only cell leaders should fill these posts, preferably cell leaders who have multiplied their cells. As your church grows, you can then ask staff members to fill each block. It is essential that the senior pastor take at least one segment. He must not delegate this area. The senior pastor must lead the charge, practically demonstrating the priority of fervent prayer. Your prayer schedule may look like this:

- 6-9 A.M.: Senior pastor in charge
- 9-12 A.M.: Key leader in charge
- 12-3 P.M.: Church board member in charge
- 3-6 P.M.: Key leader in charge
- 6-9 P.M.: Key leader in charge
- 9-12 P.M.: Church board member in charge

The three-hour prayer block can be divided into worship, prayer for individual needs, prayer for church needs, and prayer for the country, the nation, and the world. I like to keep the group together during the time when I lead. Other pastors divide the larger group into smaller groups. Wagner's advice about praying in a group makes sense to me: "It is much wiser to stay with the least common denominator and keep the large group as a large group."[2]

Wagner acknowledges that breaking up for the purpose of sharing intimate prayer requests can sometimes be beneficial, but it can also make the prayer meeting seem mechanical and impose on people who would rather not break up into smaller groups.

There is no right or wrong way to lead these prayer segments. The right way is what works for you. I do, however, have some suggestions:

- It is a good idea to make a list of prayer requests. These hand-outs can be distributed to the newcomers.

- Individual prayer requests can be shared in the group, but do not allow the sharing time to become an end in itself. Limit the sharing time and concentrate on the prayer time. One way to avoid filling all of your time with personal prayer requests is to ask each person to pray their own prayer requests out loud and then recommend that one or two people mention those same requests in prayer. Be sure to keep moving on to additional requests. At all times, maintain the momentum of prayer.
- Make it the goal to pray 80% of the time and talk only 20% of the time.
- Try to pray and worship non-stop for at least 45 minutes. Before starting a non-stop prayer time, explain to those present that you will be praying without stopping for 45 minutes (sometimes it lasts longer.) Grant them liberty to pick a song, read a Scripture, pray more than once, etc.
- After a period of non-stop prayer, allow newcomers to introduce themselves. Some people will need to leave at this time. Normally, there is a constant flow of people as some enter and others go. The one constant is that the key leader or pastor remains.

Initially, we offered a 24-hour prayer vigil every three months, but we craved more of God's presence. If you plan to implement this strategy, consider starting slowly, meeting every quarter, and then easing into a monthly prayer time with the goal of providing a weekly prayer watch.

Let me warn you that you will not turn back the clock once you have tasted the benefits of a weekly prayer time. Since converting to a weekly prayer watch, we have experienced new growth, protection, and power in our church. You will too. God promises it: "If my people, who are called by my name, will humble themselves and pray and seek my face and turn from their wicked ways, then will I hear from heaven and will forgive their sin and will heal their land" (2 Chronicles 7:14). God will provide new protection, new liberty, and a new atmosphere. Revivals start when God's people seek His face earnestly. God wants to do the same for you and your church if you will seek Him.

Again, effective leadership is the key to making this work. The foot soldiers will follow their commanding officers, but they lose heart when leadership disappears. We have made it a rule that our staff pastors must be present for their full three-hour block, unless sickness or death gets in the way. We believe strongly in delegation, but not in this area of ministry. Even if no one from the congregation shows up, the pastor is on his knees praying.

We tell our pastors to turn off their cell phones and cancel their appointments during this time. Intercession is a serious undertaking, and we know that satan will do everything possible to distract, divert, and lead astray. We try to avoid being too rigid and under rare circumstances, a pastor might ask a layperson to replace him, but it is definitely the exception and not the norm.

I like this prayer methodology so much because it maximizes freedom and flexibility. The career person who rushes off to work in the morning can pray in the evening. The housewife who needs the extra time to prepare herself and children in the morning can visit the church mid-day when the children are in the school.

We want as many people as possible to attend our day-long Friday prayer meeting and really emphasize the meeting in church, but this is one area that we emphasize quality over quantity. We are encouraged by the fact that even if only the pastor is in the church praying, we know that God will answer his prayers and that a new, fresh anointing will descend on our church.

We originally held these prayer meetings in the sanctuary but circumstances caused us to change the location. Now we meet in a designated room that we call the 'prayer room.' It can hold approximately 20 people and there are normally between five and fifteen people praying during each three-hour segment.

I recognize that holding a three-hour segment of prayer can be daunting to anyone, especially a lay person. The leader of each part must be directive: asking individuals to pray, waiting in silence, singing praise choruses, sharing Bible verses, and allowing various people to express their burdens. The routinization of the prayer time is by far a greater danger than the fear of the unknown. Part of the prayer process is to allow the dynamic of God's Holy Spirit to break through.

Morning Prayer Meeting(s)

In 1996, I visited ICM for 10 days. The church allowed me to stay in a converted sound room in the main sanctuary. The sound room was rather large, so the church converted it into an apartment overlooking the stage. I could see everything and everyone in the church.

During those ten days, I didn't need to use an alarm clock to wake-up in the morning. Every morning at 5 A.M. I woke up to worship choruses singing: "Jesus, I love you, I praise You, I adore You," in Spanish. It did not matter when I got to bed at night. I was awakened at 5 A.M.

At ICM, the first prayer meeting starts at 5 A.M. every day. Then another group of prayer warriors enter the church at 6 A.M.; another at 7 A.M. At 10 A.M., the last group finally leaves. Back in 1996, there were probably 500 people who prayed every morning, although that number is much larger today. ICM also hosts an all-night prayer meeting every Friday. The secret to the success of ICM is dependence on God through prayer.

At Yoido Full Gospel Church in Seoul, Korea, the faithful arrive for prayer at 5:30 A.M. and they have a rotation similar to ICM's. People are encouraged to come and pray every morning. I remember one April morning when I visited the YFGC prayer meeting. That Monday, it was below freezing, ready to snow. I bundled up and went down to the main sanctuary at 5:30 A.M. There I saw 3000 Korean saints crying out to God, "Give us Korea for Your Son Jesus, dear Lord." I was amazed. I realized the largest church in the history of Christianity was a praying church. This church was willing to pay the price in prayer, and God was mightily blessing them as a result.

The early morning prayer session is a great way to get your church praying, if you can mobilize your members to attend. The early morning schedule works well for many people, even if it means only staying for a short while.

Twenty-four Hour Prayer Sign-up

One way to make prayer convenient for your church members is to allow them to pray at home in an organized fashion. A 24-hour per day sign up promotes personal prayer and ministers to the needs of the congregation.

This type of prayer is especially effective when you want your church to pray for specific requests—a harvest event in the church, reaching the goal of a specific number of cells, or just a fresh touch from God. Ask members to sign up on a list to pray for particular needs on a non-stop basis. I would recommend asking each cell member to pray for half an hour, which means that you will need a total of forty-eight people praying. Administration of the various time slots is easier if the list is posted during the celebration service, preferably at the cell group information table.[3]

Spontaneous Prayer Chains

Prayer chains are an excellent strategy to promote in your church. They are easy to start and work well in the background. In other words, prayer chains do not require individual church members to come to the church in order to pray. They work just as well at home, at work, or at school. How do you make a prayer chain work? First, promote prayer chains at the cell group level. Each cell group will distribute names and phone numbers. Then, when a need arises, one cell member will call another cell member and the cycle will continue until everyone is contacted. Unlike the twenty-four hour prayer sign up, prayer chains are best administrated at the cell group level.

All-night or Half-night Prayer Meeting

All-night prayer meetings were quite common among the cell churches that I studied. Following the model of Yoido Full Gospel Church, most of the growing cell churches in the world hold regular all-night prayer meetings. There are a wide variety of formats for this model, so I suggest that you use your creativity. Here is a basic format:

- 8:00 P.M. Dynamic worship
- 9:00 P.M. Meditation from the Word of God
- 9:45 P.M. Individual meditation and confession of sin
- 10:15 P.M. Break into groups of four to pray for personal needs
- 10:45 P.M. Pray as a group for church needs
- 11:15 P.M. Pray as a group for the nations
- 12:00 A.M. Repeat the process until 6 A.M.

Prayer Retreats

You might want to establish prayer retreats in your church. The focus of such retreats is fervent prayer. Everything is centered around seeking the living God for His blessing. YFGC has created an entire mountain called Prayer Mountain. They converted a cemetery into a place of prayer and carved out hundreds of individual caves into the mountainside. At the mountain they have a chapel—without seats, lodging for those on prayer journeys, or a restaurant—to help those praying focus on Christ. YFGC takes the spiritual battle seriously and has prepared diligently to sustain the prayer dynamic over a long period. A bus leaves every half-hour from the mother church and transports prayer warriors to Prayer Mountain.

PROMOTE PRAYER IN THE CELL GROUP

Praying cell groups are effective cell groups. The first place to promote prayer is in the cell group itself. Cell group leaders need reminders that the cell group is not primarily a social time. Successful cell groups, rather, are flowing with the presence of God. The presence of Jesus Christ is the key to cell group success. An ordinary cell group:

1. *Begins with prayer.* The cell leader asks Jesus to fill the cell with His presence (or better yet, asks someone in the group to open in prayer.)
2. *Draws members into God's presence during worship.* Worship is a deep act of approaching the living God. It is also a form of prayer.
3. *Intersperses prayer in the worship and before the lesson.* One of the best ways to get people praying is to ask them to pray between songs. Call on individual members, but not newcomers, to pray out loud between the songs. Try to vary this time. During a normal worship time in my small group, we sing a few songs without interruption, I ask different people to pray out loud, and then we have a time of silent meditation. I never follow a rote order, but rather depend on the Spirit of God to lead the group.
4. *Has members who pray for one another after the lesson.* God's Word often pinpoints areas of need. Be careful not to shorten the prayer time because of a long lesson. I have discovered that

prayer requests often naturally surface during the lesson time that a cell leader can later cover in the prayer request time.

5. *Shows sensitivity to spontaneous prayer requests.* I remember one cell that I visited. The leader asked each member to pick his or her favorite worship song. One member named Theresa picked a song about renewal. After singing the song, Theresa began to sob saying, "I picked that song because I desperately need renewal in my life. My non-Christian husband is talking about leaving me and he's treating me like dirt. I really need all of you tonight. Please pray for me." Immediately, the cell group surrounded her and began lifting her up before the throne of God. Theresa left the cell group that evening completely renewed.

6. *Has members who pray for newcomers to attend the cell during the vision casting time.* Bethany World Prayer Center in Baker, Louisiana and Faith Community Baptist Church in Singapore have popularized the practice of writing down the names of non-Christians and persistently praying for them to attend the cell group. This is a helpful practice that I wholeheartedly endorse. If your church does, I recommend using small white boards to write down the names of non-Christian friends and relatives. Be sure to hide the white boards when those non-Christians visit your groups to avoid offending them.

INDIVIDUAL PRAYER

Spiritually strong cell group leaders are the most effective cell group leaders. We must remember that leadership is not by might, nor by power, but by the Spirit of God. I constantly tell my cell leaders to stop preparing the cell lesson at least half an hour before the cell meeting starts. Why? So that they will seek God and ask for His blessings on their cell groups.

True success in cell groups and cell churches comes from God. The secret is not the cell structure, the cell order, or the cell pastor—it is the blessing of the Almighty God upon the congregation. God spoke to Jeremiah saying, "But let him who boasts boast about this: that he understands and knows me, that I am the LORD, who exercises kindness, justice and righteousness on earth, for in these I delight," (Jeremiah 9:24). I encourage churches to spot, develop, and release spiritual people—those who depend on God and know how to seek His face. Other leadership characteristics can help but spirituality is the chief requirement.

Some have accused the G-12 strategy as being nothing more than a Christian pyramid system. Nothing could be further from the truth. I remember talking to a very successful multi-level marketing man who had made millions. This man converted to Christianity and happened to come in contact with one of the largest G-12 churches in the world. He felt he could build a large church because of his experience in business. He soon discovered, however, that he lacked the spiritual power to make it work. It was not about following the latest technique. When I spoke with him, he had failed miserably and was on his knees before God asking for His special guidance. He realized that he had to pay the price in prayer to gain the needed power.

JUST DO IT

After all of our struggles at the Republic Church, we had become experts at teaching on prayer without praying. We finally became tired of talking and decided to start doing. We had to commit ourselves to become doers. My advice is to start doing something. You might need to adjust along the way, but start doing something.

The key question that you must ask yourself is this: are we praying? If you cannot say yes to this question, I give you three words of advice—Just Do It. The most important thing is not that you do it right, but that you do something. Some people criticized D.L. Moody for his bold style of evangelism. The evangelist responded, "You might be right, but I prefer what I'm doing to what you're not doing." Prayer methodologies and strategies abound. But none of them matter if you are not actually praying as a church.

7

CAPTURING

A CONTAGIOUS VISION

When César Fajardo started the youth ministry at ICM in 1987, there were only 30 young people. He began to dream of reaching the lost youth of Bogota. When he preached, he imagined that the place was filled. He openly declared to his small group, "There will come a time when young people will have to line-up to enter this church." In 1987, Fajardo took a photograph of the nearby indoor stadium full of people. He then hung that photograph on the wall in his room and began to dream and believe God to fill it with young people.[1]

I weep every time I attend a youth service at ICM. Over 20,000 young people worshipping Jesus. Ex-drug addicts. Guerilla fighters. Broken people. All eyes are on Jesus.

God is pleased when we attempt great things for His glory and we expect great things from Him. Jesus tells us that all authority is given to Him (Matthew 28:18-20). Before we can begin doing great things, we need to envision what God wants to do in our city and our nation.

Is your vision contagious? Does it grab you, grip you, and ultimately infect others? Is it like a spreading virus to those around you?

EVERYONE A MINISTER

Jesus freed us to serve—not sit. John writes, "To him who loves us and has freed us from our sins by his blood, and has made us to be a kingdom and priests to serve his God and Father—to him be glory and power for ever and ever! Amen" (Revelation 1:5-6). The most dynamic principle that we can learn is that the harvest is too big for one person:

> When Jesus saw the crowds, he had compassion on them, because they were harassed and helpless, like sheep without a shepherd. Then he said to his disciples, 'The harvest is plentiful but the workers are few. Ask the Lord of the harvest, therefore, to send out workers into his harvest field.' He called his twelve disciples to him and gave them authority to drive out evil spirits and to heal every disease and sickness (Matthew 9:36-10:1).

The vision to reach a world for Jesus must compel us to see everyone as a potential harvest worker.

The fastest growing cell churches in the world believe that cell ministry is the best way to evangelize and disciple others. ICM, for example, asks everyone to enter the cell leadership training process to eventually lead a cell group, reproduce the cell group, and disciple the daughter cell leaders. The secret to ICM's success is that they have created a cell group leader movement—a leadership explosion.

ICM views leading a cell as the natural process of spiritual maturity (e.g., gathering one's friends, evangelizing, discipling, etc.).

Does everyone become a leader? No. But I can assure you that many more do because of ICM's pragmatic stance. Now, if they would have said, "Only those who feel a calling should become cell leaders," we would not even be talking about ICM today. The vision that anyone can become a leader is contagious.

Pastor Obajah, the pastor of GBI (also called the Family of God Church), one of the largest cell churches in Indonesia, learned about the G-12 structure when he visited ICM in the late 1990s. He could not speak a word of Spanish or English, but he went back to Indonesia with one important principle: every person is a potential leader.

He started his equipping track with the goal of preparing everyone in the church to become a cell group leader. He encouraged the spirit of leadership in his church, and this principle struck such a fire that his church has grown to 1,500 cell groups and 15,000 members. Many people all over Indonesia and Asia now attend conferences at GBI.[2]

When I taught in Pastor Obajah's church in 2001, I noticed that whenever Pastor Obajah spoke, he highlighted one major theme: anyone can be a cell leader. He gave example after example of ordinary people leading cell groups: rickshaw drivers, uneducated people, and even children!

Lon Vining, cell church planter to a post-modern community in North America, explains it this way:

> I think that those who have advocated an equipping track that ends in 'everyone becoming a cell group leader' have done so with the idea of raising the bar. I think they are trying to say, in essence, that instead of cell group leadership being 'for highly-trained ministry specialists,' or 'super-spiritual Christians,' (an elite few), that instead, cell leadership (and the type of disciple that fits that profile) is something much more

closer to the NORM of Christian life as one matures. The track ending there also indicates to the general congregation that it's a spiritual goal that is reachable by many, not just a few. From a practical standpoint, it seems like it would be hard to point people toward this goal (leading a cell group) when you don't indicate that it's the goal for everyone. Some people, who just underestimate themselves, may 'opt out' in the beginning and never 'push to the top' unless they are put on track to begin the process of becoming a cell leader in the beginning.[3]

Sometimes the word 'leader' hinders us from thinking that anyone can truly be one, but the issue we are really talking about is spiritual parenthood. It is part of the maturing process. Maturity does not come from sitting on the sidelines; it comes from being involved in the game.

How many parents do you know that felt like they were ready for parenthood? Most of them would tell you they learned through having children. Leading a cell group and caring for cell members is the same way. We develop spiritual muscles as we serve. Mark Goodge, a leader in the cell church movement, said this,

No one would suggest, for example, that some men are more qualified and/or gifted to be the head of the household in their own home than others. That's just part of the territory that goes with being a husband and father. You don't need special training or gifting, you just do it. Of all the various comparisons that can be made, I would say that cell leadership comes closest to being 'head of the household' in the context of the cell. Sure, there are ways to improve, and ways to learn how to be more effective in what you do, but that simply means making the most of the abilities you already possess rather than seeking out completely new ones.[4]

Some people think it is wrong to ask everyone to eventually lead a cell group. They say that not everyone has a gift for leading a cell group. I used to think this way until God and statistics showed me otherwise.[5] Many of you reading this book will have already read my first book, *Home Cell Group Explosion* (TOUCH Publications, 1998), which reveals research about how anyone can successfully lead and multiply a cell group. I now teach that everyone *can* lead a cell group, although not everyone *will* lead a cell group.

Scott Boren, Director of Publishing and Research at TOUCH Publications, has developed a continuum of spiritual growth from a lost person to church leader that looks like this:

• Observer of Christian community
• Worshipper at celebration
• Participant in cell life
• Servant doing activities in a cell group
• Person of influence leading a cell group
• Mentor developing other cell group leaders[6]

As soon as we look only for the brightest and the best to lead cell groups, or only those with the gift of leadership, we will severely limit our pool of leaders and short-change those under us.

FREEDOM FROM SIN

Paul tell us in Titus 2:11-16: "For the grace of God has appeared, bringing salvation to all men, instructing us to deny ungodliness and worldly desires and to live sensibly, righteously and godly in the present age, looking for the blessed hope and the appearing of the glory of our great God and Savior, Christ Jesus; who gave Himself for us, that He might redeem us from every lawless deed and purify for Himself a people for His own possession, zealous for good deeds."

We often associate grace with salvation from sin. And yes, salvation by grace is the blessed message of the Reformation. Martin Luther realized that he could never earn his salvation and finally received by faith the gospel of grace.

Yet we also must remember that God's grace sanctifies us. It teaches us to say no to sin and ungodliness. It transforms us and makes us holy. Pastor Castellanos says, "When there is sin, the cell group will fall. If someone is living with someone outside of marriage, you must not allow such a person to lead a cell group. Holiness must begin with the leader."[7] Claudia Castellanos says that in order to multiply cell groups you have to obey the Word of God, be committed to holiness, have a healed heart, and receive liberation. These steps are the key to an abundant multiplication.[8]

I am a firm believer that every potential cell group leader must be thoroughly set free from past sins before leading a cell groups. Fruitfulness in service depends on a person being set free from spiritual, emotional, and physical bondages.

IMMEDIATE FOLLOW-UP AND PREPARATION

Many people who attend the services at ICM see the crowds, but fail to see the disciples. They do not realize that ICM has a superb method of taking a new believer from A to B. The different stages look something like this:

- Convert to Christianity
- Become a cell group member
- Attend an Encounter Retreat (including classes before and after)
- Go through training (the School of Leaders)
- Lead a cell group (normally after the second Encounter retreat)
- Multiply the cell group and care for the new leaders

Let us look closely at the underlying principles that ICM applies to see how they might work in your church.

Every cell group leader is a potential supervisor.

To make the absolute goal *cell group leadership* would short-sight the vision and cause it to stagnate, maybe even die. You must give people a vision beyond themselves. Help them to believe that they will eventually become leaders of leaders. As I have shared earlier, give them an initial vision of leading a cell and multiplying it three times. In most countries I think this is a wise, practical thing to do.

Perhaps the delicate point here is making sure that the future goal is neither too high nor too low. If it is too high, people say, "When the Lord wants to do that thing, let Him." If it is too low, people ask, "What's the big deal?"

This is vision casting; this is dreaming. This is believing the eternal God who "...calls things that are not as though they were" (Romans 4:17 b). Supervising, pastoring, and discipling a daughter cell leader unwraps core spiritual muscles deep within. It stirs people to help others succeed. From this group, some will even decide to enter the ministry.

There is a hunger for church growth.

Those churches that reap the harvest realize that the harvest is far too great for any one person. They take heed to the words of Jesus when He tells us to pray to the Lord of the harvest to send forth workers into his harvest field. The vision for church growth flows from Christ's compassion on the multitudes:

> He had compassion on them, because they were harassed and helpless, like sheep without a shepherd. Then he said to his disciples, 'The harvest is plentiful but the workers are few. Ask the Lord of the harvest, therefore, to send out workers into his harvest field.' He called his twelve disciples to him and gave them authority to drive out evil spirits and to heal every disease and sickness (Matthew 9:36-10:1).

God used Matthew 9:35-10:1 to speak directly to Pastor Castellanos about the need to raise up disciples to reap the harvest. Church growth is highly valued and esteemed at ICM. Pastor Castellanos says, "Some people talk about wanting only quality and not quantity. But God is concerned about both—quality and quantity. The church that doesn't grow is like stagnated water. The church that doesn't grow begins to turn in on itself and sows all kinds of wickedness."[9] He goes on to say,

> A church must not start in January with a certain number and have the same number by the end of December...this is a reflection that the church is not fulfilling the great commission. This type of fruitlessness normally occurs in churches that are loaded down with programs that absorb their energy but don't produce evangelistic results...[10]

We must not expect all churches around the world to experience the same type of dynamic growth. The fact is that most churches are growing in Colombia because the soil is ready and God is producing the harvest. Church growth in Thailand, for example, is totally different. When I held a cell seminar in Thailand, I rarely talked about the huge throngs of Colombia because it would have discouraged them.

Yet, even in Thailand, the most fruitful churches are the ones who long after church growth, pray for it, prepare for it, and do what it takes to see it happen. Will the growth be slower in Thailand? No doubt about it. But this should not quench the fire to see more people converted, discipled, and sent out.

North America is quickly becoming a mission field. In North America, "It takes the combined efforts of eighty-five Christians working over an entire year to produce one convert. At that rate, a huge percentage of people will never have the opportunity, even once, to hear the gospel in a way they can understand it from a friend they trust."[11]

This should stir us even more to cry mightily out to God. We must believe that God wants churches to grow and for this reason, we must catch the vision of a great harvest. We must see that cell groups are the best way to grow in number without losing quality.

THE EARLY CHURCH REVOLUTION

Jesus concentrated on His disciples. He realized that winning one or two scattered sheep would not create a movement. He needed harvest workers. When Jesus died, he left behind a team of laborers that continued His work in the face of fierce persecution. They did not have elaborate buildings, power, money, or prestige at their command. They met in believers' homes, celebrating together when it was possible for them to do so.

Because the church viewed every person as a potential laborer involved in harvesting and starting churches, the gospel of the kingdom radically impacted society. When the church fell into the hands of a select few, it lost its power, its effectiveness, and it was thrust into the dark ages. The cell church philosophy combined with the application of G-12 principles helps us more fully realize the New Testament ideal of "everyone a minister." In a church where the G-12 principles are in full gear, there is a earnest zeal to convert every hearer into a doer, every pew-sitter into a servant-leader.

8

CAUGHT

IN THE NET

Jesus told Peter, "Put out into deep water, and let down the nets for a catch" (Luke 5:4). Peter obeyed and reaped the fruit: "When they had done so, they caught such a large number of fish that their nets began to break. So they signaled their partners in the other boat to come and help them, and they came and filled both boats so full that they began to sink…then Jesus said to Simon, 'Don't be afraid; from now on you will catch men'" (Luke 5:7-10). Peter was not fishing by himself using a pole. Rather, he was accompanied by a team of people using nets.

Four words have motivated the vision of many churches using G-12 principles to reach out to non-believers: Win, Consolidate, Disciple, and Send.[1] Using these principles within the context of a cell church team will allow your nets to catch many fish.

WIN

The first step requires winning others to Jesus. As He told His disciples,

Do you not say, 'Four months more and then the harvest?' I tell you, open your eyes and look at the fields! They are ripe for harvest. Even now the reaper draws his wages, even now he harvests the crop for eternal life, so that the sower and the reaper may be glad together. Thus the saying 'One sows and another reaps' is true. I sent you to reap what you have not worked for. Others have done the hard work, and you have reaped the benefits of their labor (John 4:35-38).

Every method available should be used to lead others to Jesus. The cell church is perfectly positioned to extend both its arms, the cell group and the celebration, to reach a hurting world for Jesus. The image of sowing and reaping perfectly suits the cell church. Every cell member sows a seed when reaching out to neighbors, family, and friends. Eventually, the cell group reaps the harvest by actually winning them to Christ.

CONSOLIDATE

After winning new believers to Jesus, the next step is consolidation. The basic principle of consolidation is a refusal to allow newly won believers to slip away from their new lives in Christ. Once caught, the fish must not be let back into the ocean to swim away.

Immediate Follow-up

After Pastor Eddy Leo of the Abbalove Church in Jakarta, Indonesia visited ICM in 1998, he decided that the growth at ICM was more a result of their excellent follow-up system than of their precise G-12 model. Pastor Leo took the principle of consolidation at ICM and adapted it to fit his congregation's needs. What the Abbalove Church does now is to usher each new believer into a Welcome Room where a counselor discusses with her the assurance of salvation.

That very same week, a cell group from the same district prays for the new believer, and then a cell member contacts her, asking about her needs and saying the group is praying and would like to visit. Normally, someone other than the friend who brought her to church would be rejected. But because the focus is on caring for felt needs, the door is opened. Generally, the visiting cell member makes four visits in the first four weeks, explaining to the new believer how to grow in Christ and inviting her to attend the cell group.

The focus is on *connection*, connecting a new believer to someone else and making sure that the connection is not broken. Adapting this principle to your church's situation will involve making corrections and adjustments until it actually works. How will you know when it is working? When the newly saved begin attending a cell group and then go on to the pre-encounter.

Pre-encounter

A pre-encounter is a series of two to five classes that focus on preparing people for the Encounter Retreat. Because many who attend an Encounter Retreat are new to the work of God's Spirit, pre-encounter classes will include teaching on basic Christian doctrine and the need to be set free from sin. It will also teach people what to expect in the actual Encounter Retreat.

When I led the first encounter retreat at The Light Church, I learned the importance of holding pre-encounter classes. During the first retreat, we had to spend a lot of time educating people that the Encounter Retreat was more than a series of Bible sermons or a recreational event. Some participants even resisted the deeper life-teaching because we did not prepare them beforehand.

Encounter God

The keystone in the consolidation process is seeing that new believer attending an Encounter Retreat. Justin Mulder, a youth pastor in South Africa, said, "My own feeling on why people don't become cell leaders is that they are weighed down by personal baggage which they are not delivered from."[2] An Encounter Retreat will enable new Christians to break through their bondage to sin and be released free and whole again. In so doing, they will be more prepared to consider the training for cell group leadership.

Weekend retreat training is not a new concept. Dion Robert, senior pastor of the more than 120,000 member Works and Mission Baptist Church in Abidjan, Ivory Coast, has used Encounter Retreats for many years, long before other cell church pioneers. Pastor Robert calls Encounter Retreats 'soul therapy.'

The salvation promised by Jesus Christ involves our entire being: body, soul, and spirit.[3] The work of the church must therefore be concerned with this whole being, just as the Bible says in 1 Thessalonians 5:23: "May God himself, the God of peace, sanctify you through and through. May your whole spirit, soul, and body be kept blameless at the coming of our Lord Jesus Christ."

Jesus said: "The Spirit of the Sovereign Lord is on me, because the Lord has anointed me to preach good news to the poor. He has sent me to bind up the brokenhearted, to proclaim freedom for the captives and release from darkness for the prisoners, to proclaim the year of the Lord's favor..." (Isaiah 61:1-2a; Luke 4:18-19). Christ's words contain very practical advice for soul therapy. After God sent Him to announce the good news to the poor and proclaim the year of the Lord's favor, Jesus tells us that He came:

- To bind up the brokenhearted.
- To proclaim freedom for the captives.
- To proclaim release for the prisoners.

Soul therapy requires a spiritual battle. As Paul says in 2 Corinthians 10:3-5, "For though we live in the world, we do not wage war as the world does. The weapons we fight with are not the weapons of the world. On the contrary, they have divine power to demolish strongholds. We demolish arguments and every pretension that sets itself up against the knowledge of God, and we take captive every thought to make it obedient to Christ."

The power of an Encounter Retreat to wage those spiritual battles is now available to the church thanks to Pastor Jim Egli's groundbreaking research on Encounter Retreats. This material, which includes PowerPoint© presentations and workbooks, is available in an eight part video series called *Encounter God.*[4]

The purpose of this excellent resource is to instruct people to lead Encounter Retreats. Adding Encounter Retreats to your church's training arsenal is now both possible and practical. Pastor Egli presents several important themes:

- Understanding Spiritual Warfare (teaching on the power of sin and how to break that power)
- From Darkness to Light (focuses on liberation from occult bondage)
- From Bondage to Freedom (focuses on liberation from the sins of the flesh)
- From Impure to Pure (focuses on dealing with sexual strongholds)
- From Broken to Whole (focuses on learning to forgive others)
- From Rebellion to Submission (focuses on liberation from rebellious attitudes)

• From Cursing to Blessing (focuses on breaking curses over our lives)
• Living in Victory (emphasizes maintaining a close walk with Jesus)

The teaching in these eight sessions gets right to the heart of the matter: the need to be holy as God Himself is holy.

Bethany World Prayer Center also has excellent material called *Encounter Retreat: Breaking the Chains that Bind* (BCCN, 2002). Bethany's Encounter follows the ICM Encounter model and has seen many lives transformed through their retreats.

Regardless of which materials your church decides to use or create, there are some key principles necessary for success.

Preparation for the Encounter

The amount of preparation put into an Encounter Retreat will determine its results. A hurried, unplanned Encounter will lead to frustration. It is a good idea to begin preparing three months in advance for the Encounter Retreat. The first place to start is in prayer. God will not only prepare the hearts of the participants beforehand, but He will also remind you, the planner, of what you will need to do. Things to consider:

• Who will lead worship?
• Where will the people eat? Sleep?
• What program will the Retreat follow?
• Who will serve as spiritual counselors?

It is usually best to hold the Encounter Retreats by gender, but if you cannot because of the size of your church, remember to divide groups by gender during the application sessions.

Get Away

It is tempting to hold an Encounter Retreat in the church building, but you should be aware of some pitfalls. While a local retreat might be more convenient for church members, the natural tendency for those attending is to maintain *some* appointments, see *certain* people, and fulfill a *limited number* of commitments. The coming and going leads to a lack of concentration that hinders the work of the Holy Spirit's work in the lives of all participants. Instead of holding the Encounter Retreat at the church, get away to a retreat center. The focus should be on one thing: God's powerful work. It is a commitment that will cost more, but the fruit will far exceed the sacrifice.

Get Away Long Enough

Many encounters start on Friday evening and finish on Saturday evening, though I recommend holding the first post-Encounter session that Sunday afternoon. If you can do this, you will get the best results. Pastor Jim Egli, an expert on this subject, says,

> We have done short ones (Friday evening and Saturday morning and afternoon) and also done ones that went into Sunday. I am convinced that at least here in the US the ideal length is to go into Saturday evening. We consistently were told that the retreat was too short when we ended Saturday. afternoon. Now that we end Saturday evening it seems just right. I have also led one that went through Sunday afternoon. Of course you can cover more and the schedule isn't so tight but I don't think that it is worth the extra expense and the extra time commitment. We begin on Friday at 7:00 or 7:30 or so and we end on Saturday evening.[5]

Avoid Legalism

People naturally want to know what constitutes a sin and what does not. Speaking to the group of thirty-five people who gathered for my first Encounter Retreat, I noticed the tendency of people to ask specific questions like, "Is it wrong to watch pro-wrestling?" However, categorizing sin will result in legalism. Avoid playing Holy Spirit-instead allow God to reveal the wrongs of others. Remind people to be sensitive to the Holy Spirit in order to focus on the things that are obviously wrong. Do not pressure people to confess anything they are not prepared to confess.

Post-encounter

Post-encounter teaching takes place immediately after the retreat. Those who have attended the Encounter Retreat need further training. The Encounter Retreat creates the hunger in people to learn more. The post-encounter, like the pre-encounter, is a series of lessons that help each encounter participant continue to grow in Christ.

Immediate Induction into Further Training

The days and weeks following an Encounter Retreat are exciting ones for those people who participated. As a church, you need to harness that excitement and use it to drive your church's vision by connecting the Encounter Retreat to the remainder of your church's training. Otherwise, your church can become so excited about what happened on the retreat that you fail to continue the new believers on their journey toward the ultimate goal of becoming leaders who disciples more leaders.

I know one church that became an Encounter Retreat Church! They lost their cell church vision because they became so enamored with the Encounters. Were the Encounter Retreats helpful in this church? Yes. Did they set people free? Yes. Did the people stay free? Probably not.

Remember this: Encounter Retreats must be intimately linked with the training track that follows. Resist the tendency to focus too much on the Encounter and too little on the immediate training afterward. In fact, I would recommend not beginning to hold Encounters until your church has developed a clear training track to follow immediately after each Encounter Retreat. Unless your church has clearly established its training track, there is a good chance that you will lose the fruit of your Encounter Retreat.

The last sessions of the Encounter retreat involve vision-casting that assists participants in finding their purpose in life—to become disciples and make disciples by leading cell groups, multiplying cell groups, and discipling others.

The date for the next week's training session should be posted and everyone should understand that they are expected to attend the post-encounter classes. I think the best time to start training after the retreat is that Sunday morning because it is connected to an established life-changing event.

It is also a great idea if the same group that enters the Encounter Retreat (and perhaps combined with another group, such as a women's group, that attended an Encounter on the same weekend) is immediately integrated into the training track and works toward the goal of cell group leadership together. This is more effective because there is a sense of camaraderie among fellow participants. People were set free together. They heard each other's testimony, saw the brokenness and transparency. Each person developed a sincere desire to stay free, and because they reached that point together, they will want to help each other achieve that goal. Freedom, instead of being an individualistic goal, hard to achieve when standing alone, becomes a group goal that has a greater chance of success.

Will your church have to adjust? Yes. You might even start with someone else's material. My prayer is that you will eventually follow the Spirit to the point where you will develop your own material.

DISCIPLE

The best preparation for moving toward cell leadership is to move from the Encounter Retreat to the training track. The most important question to ask about your church's training is, "Does it work?" Consider whether or not there are more people completing the training track and leading cell groups as a result of the training your church uses. Your church might be able to simply fine-tune its current cell leadership training materials in order to link them to the Encounter Retreat. If not, you will have to adapt more thoroughly or even consider purchasing new materials.

Do not worry too much about the particular training your church decides to use. Although some people feel that what makes the training work is the material, the exact teaching, or some kind of anointing, the real power comes from setting a person free from sin in a dynamic environment. Once there, the person will be able to understand why God put us here, to become a disciple and make disciples. While that person is sensitive to the Holy Spirit, training should begin and continue until he or she is leading a cell group.

The training that follows the Encounter Retreat should teach each potential leader, no longer a new believer, basic Christian doctrine, how to have a personal quiet time, how to evangelize, and how to lead a cell group. For more details, consult my book, *Leadership Explosion* (TOUCH Publications, 2000).

SEND

Sending is the natural progression after winning, consolidating, and discipling. The potential leader learned the mission of leading a cell during her first Encounter Retreat. Now, it is time to actually do it.

Remember that during the entire equipping process from winning to sending, the person has been actively involved in a cell group and has even been asked to lead each of the cell parts. The mother cell leader has been preparing the potential cell leader by following the model of Jesus:

- I do—you watch
- I do—you assist
- You do—I assist
- You do—I watch

A parent cell leader should allow his intern to watch him, then explain what he did and why he did it. Next, he should observe his intern as she does the same activity. Each parent cell leader should discuss his intern's performance, objectively explaining strengths and weaknesses that he observed. He should also provide remedial training to strengthen the weaknesses. More and more, the parent cell leader must turn his tasks over to the intern, withdrawing and using 'benign neglect.' He should remain a close friend, while treating the intern as his equal.

Once the discipleship and mentoring stage has reached the point where the intern is performing all the tasks of cell leadership, she is ready to launch a new cell group. Opening a cell is a powerful experience and should be celebrated. Those churches who follow the precise G-12 model ICM created believe that new leaders must attend a second weekend retreat before actually leading cell groups on their own. The principles behind this are to provide more training and to serve as a special commissioning event. Although your church might do things differently, make sure that you have given your new leaders all the training possible and that you celebrate the opening of the new cell groups.

Doing so ensures that the cycle of win, consolidate, disciple, and send will continue as the team of fishermen grows and begins casting larger nets farther asea.

THE NUTS AND BOLTS

OF G-12

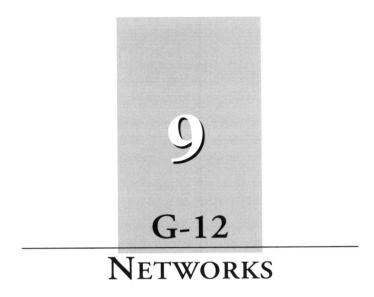

9

G-12

NETWORKS

In today's culture, people relate to one another through shared interests, work-related activities, or common needs. Extensive research has been developed on how to reach family members, close friends, and work associates regardless of where they live. The phrase *oikos evangelism* (developed primarily by Ralph Neighbour) teaches us to reach those with whom we have already established some kind of relationship. In my own small group, for example, the non-Christians we have attracted have been unsaved work associates and family members invited by core members.

GEOGRAPHICAL ORGANIZATION

Many successful cell churches around the world have chosen to organize their small group ministries geographically. Because Yoido

Full Gospel Church, which operates its cell ministry by geographical boundaries, initiated the modern cell church movement, geographical organization is the standard in the cell church world. But a new wind of change is blowing through the cell church world due to certain pitfalls of organizing cell groups geographically:

Multiplication

If geography defines who can attend a cell group, there are not as many options for multiplying those same cell groups. If the cell group has to multiply within a specific, geographically-defined area, it becomes necessary to raise up leaders and find new members who live in that particular area, which restricts who can lead the group and who can attend the new group.

Friendships

It is often more natural to reach close friends, relatives, and work associates regardless of where they live. This is not to say that reaching out to neighbors is not important. Just the opposite is true. Even so, I do not believe that it is wise to strictly organize cell ministry according to geography. Friendships are not defined geographically, so it does not make sense for cell groups to be. Because of this conviction, I have never organized a small group ministry geographically. My only experience in cell ministry has been with homogeneous groups, because I have always felt this was the best way.

Our cells are primarily organized as family cells, young married cells, women's cells, men's cells, professional cells, youth cells, adolescent cells, and children's cells. The bread and butter category was always family cells. As the church grew, we added staff to oversee each category.

HOMOGENEOUS NETWORKS

The word homogeneous means similar in nature. Homogeneous cell groups are comprised of people with common characteristics. The most common types of homogeneous groups are

- Family cell groups
- Young married couples' cell groups
- Men's cell groups
- Women's cell groups
- Singles' cell groups
- Adolescent cell groups
- University cell groups
- High school cell groups
- Children's cell groups

The list above is provided to reveal the possibilities; these are not fixed groupings that must exist in a church.

If you choose to organize according to homogeneity, it is best to call the cell groupings 'networks' because it describes their interconnectedness and cohesiveness. A network is a group of people that communicate with one another and work together as a unit or system of units. As the cell groups grow in a church, networks of groups will develop. For instance, a men's cell group will develop into other men's groups that will eventually form a men's network.

HOMOGENEOUS FLEXIBILITY

Our homogeneous categories flowed naturally from the gifts, personalities, and burdens of each pastor. For example, one of our pastors had a burden for young married couples. We gave him the liberty to start cells among the young married couples, but we also made it clear that we were not going to give him authority over every young married couple that entered the church. This was a general category, not a rigid one.

Another example was our network of women's cell groups. For awhile, the senior pastor's wife took over this network, but she never felt a strong calling to do this. For this reason, we decided that it was best to discontinue a separate homogeneous network called 'women's cells.' Rather, we decided to allow both women's cells and men's cells to start naturally within each network. We always had a number of women's and men's cells, but we didn't categorize them under a particular network called the 'women's cell network' or the 'men's cell network.'

We were flexible in formulating our homogeneous networks. We never liked to say that we had arrived at one—and only one— particular strategy or definition. As our networks grew, we continued to adapt and change the homogeneity of each network.

HOW STRICT MUST YOUR CHURCH BECOME?

One pastor wrote to me,

Do you see any danger in adopting mixed-gender 12's? I know that Bethany [World Prayer Center] and [ICM in] Bogota and others seem to feel strongly that the [cell] groups should be gender-specific, and that the G-12 would naturally be too. However, our groups are not divided by gender, and if that is the case, the 12's won't easily be, either…Other reasons—in our polity we are going to have female staff (our children's director is female), and my wife does not see herself as the leader of all the ladies (she is committed to the Lord and the work, but not comfortable as a 'co-pastor') and from what I can tell, the best arrangement for gender specific 12's is the have the pastor be the leader of men, including staff, and the wife be the core leader of the females. But at this point I think we are not in a position to go that way, so I plan to go with a mixed 12…

I responded, "It is best to allow the homogeneous networks to flow naturally. Only begin new homogeneous categories as the need arises. Don't force your groups into unnatural categories, like men's groups or women's groups." I assured him that he was doing the right thing by focusing on mixed gender family cells, especially since one of the greatest problems around the world is the breakdown of the nuclear family.

The cell church worldwide is learning that strict geographical barriers often hinder rather than strengthen cell ministry, but this argument can be equally true when applied to strict homogeneous boundaries, such as men and women, or single and married.

A GREAT EXAMPLE

Cypress Creek Church (CCC) in Wimberley, Texas started in 1993 and has since grown to over 100 cell groups with more than 1000 people in attendance. Pastor Rob Campbell has visited ICM and has supercharged his church with G-12 principles, including Encounter Retreats, a School of Leaders, and team gatherings.

I was excited to see growing multiplying home cell groups among adolescents, high school students, and university students at CCC. CCC has noticed that their adolescent and young adult cell groups work best among the same gender. They discovered that it was far more effective for boys to meet with boys and girls with girls in their junior high, high school, and university cell groups. They discovered that when adolescent boys, for example, met with adolescent girls, there were too many other emotions swirling in the air to effectively minister to one another.

The youth cells at ICM in Bogota, on the other hand, are mixed gender. A young woman might even have young men in her G-12 group at ICM.[1] Pastor Campbell realized that following ICM's categories was not the key to success. He knew he had to adapt the principles to his particular situation.

At CCC, the major homogeneous category among the adults is family cell groups. Pastor Campbell is focusing on the family unit and has not felt the need to separate further into homogeneous men's cell groups or women's cell groups. CCC is impressive because it is following the Holy Spirit and adapting G-12 principles to its particular situation.

Map Out Geographical Patterns

Some churches promote geographical cell groups because of the ease of connecting newcomers with cell groups based on geographical proximity. The same principle, however, can apply to the homogeneous networks. First, color code the cells based on the particular types of networks they represent (e.g., red for youth cells; blue for family cells; green for women's cells, etc.) Second, acquire a large map and pinpoint all of the cells with colored pins. Third, place a key at the bottom of the map explaining the color code and listing meeting times, the names of cell leaders, phone numbers, and other pertinent information.

This way presents the best of both worlds. People can search the map by proximity as well as the type of homogeneous group each seeks.

Network Activities

In Chapter 4, I talked about how the G-12 structure looks from the top down. The pastor gathers his G-12 leadership team and ministers to them.

Each of the members of the pastor's G-12 are leading cells and developing a network of cells. One of them, for example, might be the person overseeing the youth cells. Let's call him Steve.

Steve has multiplied six youth cells which continue to multiply. The youth cells meet weekly outside of the church building and all the youth members attend the weekly celebration service at the church. Steve also gathers the youth together for monthly gathering. This is called a network activity or a congregational gathering. The monthly youth gathering normally includes worship and Bible teaching. Occasionally, Steve invites a Christian band, drama team, or special speaker. Steve is considering having this network activity more often.

Steve's church has decided on a uniform equipping track that all adult members are encouraged to pass through. The senior pastor has given Steve the liberty to run the same equipping track among the youth.

Network gatherings are common in the cell church. These networks flow naturally from the senior pastor's own G-12 group and then those leaders directly under the senior pastor assume responsibility for them. In the early stages of your cell church transition, you will have very little network activity. As the church grows, however, you should encourage networks to meet regularly for teaching, edification, and outreach.

10

THE TEAM
GATHERING

The YMCA played an important role in my childhood. During elementary school, I played team sports for a YMCA club called the Chargers. My teammates were my best friends both on and off the field. As friends, we knew how to work together as a team. We realized that in order to win, we had to work together. The G-12 group functions a lot like the Chargers. Unity based on friendship wins the game. The goals are different and the stakes much higher, but teamwork is still the key.

THE NORMAL TEAM MEETING

The purpose of the G-12 meeting is to minister to the ministers. It is a time when those on the front line receive special attention and encouragement. It is also a time to strengthen the bonds between mother cell leader (coach) and daughter cell leader(s).

The mother cell leader (G-12 leader) provides pastoral care, support, and coaching to the daughter cell leaders. But ministry does not always flow in just one direction; it is also a time of learning from one another. An individual daughter cell leader, for example, might have special insight that the mother cell leader (G-12 leader) lacks. Thus, this regular huddling up helps everyone stay involved.

Many pastors wonder how often their G-12 group should meet. It has been my experience that biweekly meetings are the best (every other week.) If the parent cell leader has multiplied one time, the meeting will be one-on-one. If he or she has multiplied two times, it will be a one-on-two meeting, and so forth.

Having the G-12 meeting once per month lowers the quality of time spent together because the contact is not frequent enough to deal with the troubles, burdens, and successes.

Biweekly meetings mean that that every cell leader who has birthed at least one group will be meeting each week—one time with the parent to receive ministry and one time with the daughter to give ministry. Those cell leaders who have not yet given birth will only meet every other week.

Location

G-12 meetings can take place anywhere. I suggested meeting in the church building, and in Chapter 2, I mentioned the example of Liverpool Christian Life Centre. There are good reasons for recommending this:

1. To avoid having to prepare for another trip.
2. To combine prior commitment, like a service in the church, with the G-12 meeting.
3. To make sure that the meetings actually take place.

If the church is in a rented building, or there is some other reason for not meeting at the church, by all means meet in a restaurant or a home.

Length of the meeting

There is no absolute rule on this point. I believe that a one hour or one and a half hour meeting is sufficient. Naturally, more time in prayer and ministry will raise the effectiveness of the group, but there are other considerations like family, work, and preparing for a cell meeting that must be taken into account. Consider all the relevant factors and work for a time long enough to provide excellent coverage for the G-12 group, but also a length of time that is not a burden to group members.

CONTENT

Prayer and Worship

Effective team meetings involve prayer and worship. Praying for felt needs is the heart and soul of a coaching time. Team leaders should follow-up on pastoral needs and previous requests, but also ask for current needs. This means that G-12 leaders should also ask for prayer, opening up their own lives in the process.

The Lesson

Often cell churches using the G-12 care structure will transcribe the content of the senior pastor's G-12 meeting and distribute to each individual G-12 leader. This is usually a good idea for two reasons:

1. The individual G-12 leader rarely has much time to prepare his own lesson. It is great to have material already prepared.
2. It allows the senior pastor to communicate what is on his heart with the entire leadership system. (See the appendix for two

sample lessons I have included from the Liverpool Christian Life Centre to demonstrate how this works.)

I do think it is important that liberty be granted to each individual G-12 leader to speak to the immediate issues in his or her own particular leadership team. Suppose two of the three daughter cell leaders are passing through difficult times. The G-12 leader knows this and wants to talk about God's comfort in times of trials. The G-12 lesson for the week is about evangelism, which simply does not fit the present needs. In such a case, the G-12 leader might mention the evangelism theme, but then move away from it to spend the majority of the teaching time applying Scripture to the specific needs of the group.

Quality Control

Worship, sharing prayer requests, prayer, and vision casting are vital aspects of the G-12 meeting. But after the ministry time, the G-12 leader should ask the cell group leaders about cell specifics: how did the cell group go? Were there any particular trouble areas? Perhaps others in the group could help minister to a cell group leader who is having difficulties with a talker in the group or has trouble resolving a particular conflict.

PRE-MEETING PREPARATION

Prayer

Establishing and maintaining rapport goes a long way. The most important thing a G-12 leader can do for the cell group leaders under him is to pray. This will not only help them, but it will help the G-12 leader as well. Paul said to the Colossians, "For though I am absent from you in body, I am present with you in spirit and delight to see how orderly you are and how firm your faith in Christ is" (Colossians 2:5).

When we pray daily for someone, our relationship with that person is strengthened. We develop a spiritual relationship. When we see the person physically, there is an immediate connection because the price has already been paid through prayer.

I would even encourage you to have a picture of each of your team members so you can visualize them during your times of prayer (it is a great idea to have a digital photo or scanned photo to place on your computer.)

Friendship

The goodwill present in the actual G-12 meeting will be the result of the work prior to the meeting. I am referring here to phone calls, birthday cards, encouragement on Sunday morning, or time spent sharing a cup of coffee. The most important thing you have to offer each member of your G-12 group is your sincere friendship. Your love and concern will go far beyond any teaching, anointing, or special gifts you possess.

G-12

PERMANENCY

Many churches using the G-12 care structure see the G-12 group as an unbreakable relationship similar to that between parents and children. It lasts a lifetime.[1]

The idea of permanency is a two-edged sword. On the positive side, a long-term commitment can be a great blessing. On the negative side, it might diminish a person's freedom of choice. A disciple should never feel bondage or heaviness in a G-12 group, nor should he or she feel under compulsion to remain in the same discipleship relationship permanently. A distraught pastor called me from Pennsylvania with a G-12 question:

What should I do about one of our original G-12 members? She and her husband have been faithful leaders of a cell group, but recently she's been having severe emotional problems. Recently, we asked her to stop leading her cell, and thus, we also asked her to step down from the senior pastor's G-12 team gathering. The problem became especially acute because we're having a cell leadership gathering this weekend, and we asked her not to come. She feels it's the Lord's will that she comes and even seems to be suicidal if we don't invite her because she's totally sure that it's the will of God that she attends. I don't know what to do because I've heard that the G-12 commitment is a lifetime commitment and involves laying down our lives for each other. What should I do?

I told this pastor that he made the right decision by asking her to step down both from personal cell ministry as well as the G-12 group. Separation from those pressures and a time of healing, with the prayers of her former G-12 group and cell group, could eventually lead to her restoration.

WHEN A G-12 LEADER SHOULD STEP DOWN

We know that we are Christ's disciples forever because He will never leave us or forsake us (Hebrews 13:5). But we also must remember that the word 'disciple' in the Bible is descriptive for the followers of Jesus, not for the followers of someone else. Never is the word 'disciple' used to promote personal discipleship.[2] We are called to make followers of Jesus Christ. The true mark of a disciple is the image of Christ.

The Shepherding Movement in North America went astray by promoting an unhealthy dependence between disciple and leader. Your goal as a discipler is to create in your disciple a dependence on Jesus Christ, not on yourself.

The G-12 model is a great way to organize your church in order to care for, pastor, and supervise every leader. Take great care to avoid name calling, such as "John is the disciple of Scott," "Mary is Joan's disciple," and so forth. There is no need to distinguish a person by saying, "I'm in the 12 of so-and-so." Having said this, in most circumstances the leaders under our care will remain 'permanently.' However, there are circumstances that would change this.

Sin

The G-12 leadership at churches who promote permanent discipleship do not hesitate to remove people from leadership if they are not living godly lives. Sin, such as fornication, pornography, or adultery, constitutes removal from cell group leadership or G-12 leadership. Lack of submission or rebellion might also warrant removal. Keep in mind, however, the spirit of the sinner. If he or she seeks forgiveness, do not hesitate to demonstrate God's love and mercy. Remove that person from leadership temporarily, but consider reinstating him if he conquers that sin.

Lack of fruit

A leader at ICM needs to be fruitful in multiplying cell groups if he or she wants to remain in leadership. A person who stops leading a cell group or changes his philosophy about what the cell is all about does not qualify for a G-12 group. In this case, the should step down from the G-12 leadership gathering. Before doing so, however, identify the roots of the problem and attempt to work through them.

Moving away

We live in a mobile, global society. Cell group leaders lose their jobs and must find work elsewhere. Companies switch locations. New markets beckon. Permanency might be the ideal in the G-12 group, but circumstances often dictate otherwise. It is wise to build a certain flexibility into the G-12 networks when natural changes occur, especially in a country like the United States, where people often go through several major career changes.

Personal will

G-12 groups encourage commitment but do not force commitment. Forced commitment breeds legalism and bondage. Since the vast majority of those people in G-12 teams are volunteer workers, it is impossible to force someone to stay under the same coach. Some team members might decide to leave. This is unfortunate, but a reality of life. It is best for a G-12 coach to keep a positive attitude, pray for such individuals, and move on.

IMPLEMENTING G-12.3
AT DIFFERENT STAGES

12

G-12.3 IN CELL CHURCH PLANTING

Planting a church is one of the most exciting and challenging jobs in the world. It means getting dirty, making something from nothing. I love cell church planting because you do not have to start with buildings and bucks. You start with people and a simple, New Testament format that fully utilizes the home.

A NEW CHURCH PLANT

Applying the G-12.3 structure in a new church plant is unusual because there is nothing to begin with. It is necessary to first gather the church before considering the G-12 care structure. Planting a new cell church normally means finding a core and multiplying it into a crowd, rather than trying to gather a crowd that might trickle down to a core. I encourage churches not to begin weekly Sunday morning celebrations until there are 7-10 cell groups.[1]

Do not rush into celebration services.

Allow the church plant to build roots and live underground until it is strong enough to rise to the surface. If you do not build a strong core first, you will end up with a burdensome celebration service that you will have to administer and carry. Most church plants start with a few believing couples who are committed to the work. Begin meeting in a pilot cell group with the early core members. Invite others to join you.

Those in the first cell group (pilot cell) must catch the vision of the senior pastor.

Your first cell group might meet together for one year. Be careful not to multiply too quickly because the initial members need to completely understand and believe in the values of the senior pastor. If the initial group grows too quickly through conversion growth, the church-planting pastor should multiply the group and personally lead the two distinct groups.

I would be more concerned about the quality of the group than the number of people attending in those initial months. Remember that you are laying a foundation upon which to build the entire infrastructure of the church.

Develop your training track immediately.

My advice is for you to have your training track ready from the beginning. For advice on how to prepare a training track, I would recommend reading my book *Leadership Explosion* (TOUCH Publications, 2000). Implement the training track as soon as there are enough people willing to enter it. Hold it at a different time than your cell group, since the two events are significantly different.

Remember, the goal is converting non-Christians into disciples who will multiply new disciples through the cell groups. Those who attend the cell group and show signs of commitment to the church's vision should be encouraged to enter the training track.

The senior pastor forms his G-12 group.

Eventually one or two people will complete the entire training track and open their own cell groups. When this happens, the G-12.3 strategy springs to life. The new cell leaders developed in the pilot cell should be part of the senior pastor's leadership team (G-12 group.) The senior pastor should then begin to meet with the new leaders on a separate occasion for the purpose of discipleship (see Chapters 4 and 9.)

When planting a cell church, the leadership team naturally flows from the first cell group. All daughter cell group leaders from that initial cell group become part of the G-12 of the senior pastor.

Let's say the church-planting pastor's name is Mark and his wife's name is Joy. John and Susan were part of the initial core group, as were Kyle and Nancy. Both couples completed the training track, accepted the cell church vision of Mark and Joy, and have decided to begin their own cell groups. They have both taken a few people from Mark and Joy's cell group to form their cell nuclei.

As soon as each couple starts leading its own cell group, Mark and Joy begin to meet each week in a G-12 group with John, Susan, Kyle, and Nancy that is separate from the cell group. Mark encourages the two couples to visit his open cell for fellowship and support, but he does not call that the G-12 team meeting.

Pastor Mark will also periodically visit his new daughter cell groups. He and Joy want to ensure their success. They will also work hard on building deep relationships with the two couples.

In the meanwhile, Mark and Joy will continue to lead an open cell group from which will come new leaders. When these new leaders open their own cell groups, they will then join John, Susan,

Kyle, and Nancy in the G-12 group meeting. Mark and Joy will limit their G-12 group to twelve couples because they realize that the quality of care will diminish if there are too many people in one group.

Each member of the senior pastor's G-12 group cares for three multiplication leaders.

Pastor Mark has instilled in his G-12 leaders the vision for leading a cell group and multiplying it three times. God has given them a vision to see this happen.

Take John and Susan. One year after starting their first cell group, this couple gave birth to a new cell group, of which Dave was the leader. Dave is a thirty-four-year-old single man who teaches elementary school. John and Susan continue to lead their own cell group while meeting biweekly with Dave. Apart from this regular G-12 discipleship meeting, Dave often visits John and Susan's home because he has become very dear to the family.

The senior pastor and all multiplication leaders continue to lead open cell groups.

The senior pastor must continue to lead his open cell in order to keep evangelizing as well as producing new disciples who become cell group leaders. The leaders in the pastor's G-12 group continue to lead open cell groups as well, even after they have multiplied three times and are caring for their three leaders.

I have purposely avoided discussing when to start a weekly celebration service, the type of training track to use, and other important issues. My focus here is specifically on how to begin your G-12.3 care structure in a church plant.

A CHURCH PLANT WITH SOME TRADITIONAL STRUCTURE

I coached one church that had only existed for one year when the pastor decided to transition to the cell church strategy. The church started with 100 people from another congregation and had grown to 150 people. When the church began, the focus was the Sunday morning celebration. In order to make the celebration work, the church had established a volunteer committee that led the following ministries:

- Operations
- Worship
- Children
- High School
- Middle School
- Women's Fellowship
- Nursery
- Prayer

Beyond this volunteer committee, the congregation elected a church board each year to supervise the finances and other administrative matters.

As this pastor planned the transition to the cell church model, we had to think about how he would organize his G-12.3 structure. Would he include the volunteer staff? What about those already leading a small group? I encouraged him to do the following:

Start a pilot group.

I talked with him about leading a pilot cell group, in which he would invite the key leaders to participate. I told him that down the road only those leading a cell group would take part in his G-12 team.

This pastor had a lot of authority in his church, and all of the existing leaders had already agreed to transition to the cell church strategy. The senior pastor then said to those on the volunteer committee:

> As we begin in the cell direction, leadership is everything. As leaders we must lead by example, we all know that, and this is imperative for our new direction. The principle is this: in order to function as a leader within a cell church...one must lead a cell...or at least be in a cell...I am still working on parameters as I said. My 'inner circle' if you will, will need to be cell group leaders. Yes, this is a shift, but one that must eventually be made to keep the integrity of this ministry intact. While some of you are in cells and some not, please know that you are still on the leadership team and very welcome, but I am working on a time frame by which that adjustment will need to be made or one would need to step down from leadership...over time this will be the next issue to discuss and we can discuss some of that at our next meeting as well.

Only fruitful cell leaders are part of the G-12 group.

The senior pastor made it clear that the future G-12 group would be created on the basis of fruitfulness in leading and multiplying cell groups, rather than on position, power, financial giving, or presiding over a particular ministry.

The senior pastor did not promise those people in the initial pilot group that they would become part of his G-12 group. He simply invited them to participate in the pilot group. He knew that just because a person was invited into the prototype group did not mean that the person would lead a cell group or give birth to a daughter cell group.

After six months together, those who had multiplied their cell groups began meeting in a team gathering with the senior pastor called a G-12 group.

Since the pastor was already leading an open cell group during the week, I told him that any multiplication leaders from that group could also form part of his G-12 group. Thus, there were two main sources to establish his G-12 team from: the pilot group and his open cell group.

ADJUST TO YOUR SITUATION

The two scenarios in this chapter both involve young church plants. One is a pioneer church plant that begins in a home—the G-12.3 structure flows naturally from the first cell group.

The second church plant began as a daughter church with one hundred people on Sunday morning—the G-12.3 care system involved taking existing leaders through a pilot cell group. Those who multiplied from the pilot cell form part of the senior pastor's G-12 group.

The principles remain the same although the scenarios are different. I am sure that your situation is unique. Just remember the following points:

- The senior pastor continues to lead an open cell after multiplication.
- New multiplication leaders form part of the senior pastor's initial G-12 group.
- Permanency in the pastor's initial G-12 group depends on continual fruitfulness and holiness.
- The pastor's G-12 group stops at twelve multiplication leaders.
- Those in the pastor's G-12 group seek to multiply their cell groups at least three times. They continue to lead open cell

groups while caring for their multiplication cell leaders individually and as a group. G-12 meetings occur every other week.

13

TRANSITIONING
TO THE G-12.3 STRUCTURE

I knew something was wrong on my first jog. My brand-new running shoes felt too tight on my feet. I tried wearing thinner socks and then no socks at all, but nothing seemed to help. "Well, I've already spent the money, and I can't take them back. I might as well use them," I thought. Months later, however, I could hardly walk and my right foot would swell immediately after I went jogging.

Then I finally did what I should have done at the beginning: I bought a new pair of running shoes that fit. My morning jog has once again become a delight to me, and my right foot does not hurt anymore.

What does shoe size have to do with G-12 in your church? You have to get the right fit. You have to apply the principles to your unique situation. For example:

- Some churches make the mistake of trying to implement a fully developed G-12 structure before they even transition to cells.

- Others try to convert their 5x5 structure to the G-12 system without first laying the proper groundwork.
- Still others do not adapt G-12 to their church size, trying instead to run the G-12 system like a mega-church would.

The scenarios above often happen when an overexcited pastor returns from an anointed G-12 seminar and tries to copy what he has seen in the host church. Remember the shoe illustration. Does it feel right? Does it fit your church? In this chapter, I will look at different scenarios that need individual G-12 solutions.

TRANSITIONING FROM THE 5x5 STRUCTURE

Pastor Cho at Yoido Full Gospel Church organizes his cells geographically. Most of the world's largest cell churches have at one time or another followed Pastor Cho's geographical care structure. Pastor Cho's model bases its leadership structure on the advice that Jethro gave Moses:

> But select capable men from all the people—men who fear God, trustworthy men who hate dishonest gain—and appoint them as officials over thousands, hundreds, fifties and tens. Have them serve as judges for the people at all times, but have them bring every difficult case to you; the simple cases they can decide themselves. That will make your load lighter, because they will share it with you (Exodus 18:21-22).

Some call it the 5x5 structure because a supervisor cares for five cell leaders; a zone pastor directs five supervisors and thus 25 cell leaders; and a district pastor supervises five zone pastors, overseeing approximately 125 cell leaders.[1]

The International Charismatic Mission, Faith Community Baptist Church, Bethany World Prayer Center, and the Christian Center of Guayaquil were all using the 5x5 model before they transitioned to the G-12 care structure. If you are currently following the 5x5 model or an adaptation of it, the following steps will help you as you seek to transition your church.

Ask existing pastors to participate in the senior pastor's G-12 group.

If your church already has district pastors on staff, the senior pastor should pick them as part of his G-12 group. Regardless of your previous pastoral care structure, in a cell church the senior pastor must always oversee his top cell pastors.

For example, in 1998, Centennial Road Standard Church of Brockville, Ontario transitioned their leadership structure from the 5x5 model to the G-12 model. Senior Pastor Laurence Croswell converted his staff members and their spouses into his G-12 group. Pastor Croswell began meeting with them at 5:30 A.M. every Tuesday. These key leaders soon began developing their own G-12 groups and the process then continued throughout the church.

Ask each pastor and supervisor to lead an open cell group.

I recommend that you start your transition by asking everyone to lead and multiply a cell group. One of the major problems of the 5x5 care system has been removing upper-level leadership from personal leadership of a cell group. You can reverse this trend by asking all members of your staff to lead an open cell group.

Since the G-12.3 structure teaches that lay coaches supervise three cell group leaders instead of five (while still leading their own cell groups), try to distribute the load as evenly as possible. Remember that you are in transition, so some people might still have to supervise five cell group leaders. As you produce more cell group leaders, the care load can eventually be reduced to three.

Ask pastors to care for twelve cell leaders.

The goal is to have each staff pastor care for twelve cell leaders who are in turn developing new cell leaders. What then do you do with the existing cell group leaders? Those already leading a cell group should be placed under pastors as naturally as possible. For example, suppose John was a zone pastor who had five supervisors under him. Those five supervisors should be the first five members of John's G-12 group.

After making initial decisions based on the cells that already exist, the networks should grow naturally as leaders begin to multiply their cells.

Ask cell leaders to care for three cell leaders.

Ask each cell group leader to multiply her cell three times and to care for the new multiplication leaders. Make sure she continues to lead an open cell.

Allow the homogeneous groups to develop naturally.

The beauty of the G-12 care structure is that it is flexible. As you transition to the G-12 model, you do not need to use tight homogeneous categories. Allow the cells to multiply naturally. Homogenous networks may appear on their own and then your church organize around what God is doing instead of forcing people into categories.

THE G-12.3 MODEL IN A SMALLER CHURCH

How does the G-12.3 model look in a smaller church? I am referring to a church of 50 to 150 people. In a church this size, there is normally only one person on staff: the senior pastor. It follows that the senior pastor would need to pick his twelve from among the lay people. Here are a few steps to take:

The senior pastor should gather key leaders in a pilot cell group.

I would recommend that the senior pastor begin a pilot cell group consisting of key leaders who are willing to commit to leading their own cell groups in about six months. When the members begin to multiply and start their own groups, they will become part of the senior pastor's G-12 group.

It is a good idea to include some 'movers and shakers' of the church in this pilot cell, but the pastor should pick other potential leaders as well. Each member of this pilot group must be committed to leading a weekly cell group that meets outside of the church with the goal of multiplying in one year.

The senior pastor should meet with his pilot group just like a normal cell group, being careful not to convert this into a teaching time. Teaching the training track is a separate event that should be held on another occasion such as a Sunday morning.

I would recommend that the pastor use the 4Ws in this pilot cell group (Welcome, Worship, Word, Works.) For more information, or if you are unfamiliar with this format, see my book *How to Lead a Great Cell Group Meeting* (Touch Publications, 2001).

Disciple the cell group leaders.

After the first cell group multiplies into several new groups, the senior pastor will begin to meet with the new multiplication leaders on a weekly or biweekly basis. The senior pastor will give the new leaders the lesson for each week, based on his own Sunday morning teaching. He will pour his life into these new leaders, knowing that they are helping him pastor the church. His love for them will stir them to show the same love to their daughter cell group leaders.

Ask the multiplication leaders to care for three cell group leaders.

Each member of the pastor's G-12 group will have the goal of multiplying their cell groups three times and then supervising the new multiplication leaders by meeting biweekly with them and praying for them throughout the week. They will care for their leaders to the same degree that the senior pastor has cared for them.

G-12.3 in a Medium Church

Transitioning to the G-12.3 structure in a church of 200 to 350 people is very different because of the presence of existing staff personnel and more established ministries. One church of 350 that I am currently coaching is staffed with a senior pastor, a youth pastor, a children's director, and an administrator. Here is the format we used:

The pastor leads a pilot cell group with the staff.

I encouraged the pastor to lead a pilot group with his staff in a home. We thought it should last approximately six months. He agreed that his staff needed to see a real cell group in action.

Each staff member leads an open cell group.

After the staff members had seen and experienced a normal cell group, they were encouraged to gather a core team and lead a weekly, open cell group meeting outside the church.[2]

Each staff member develops a network of cell groups.

Each staff member will eventually have a network of cell groups. Thus, the primary identification of each pastor would be: Pastor So-and-so over the family cell group network, youth network, or another network. Each staff pastor would also continue to be in charge of a ministry responsibility (missions, Christian education, etc.)

The senior pastor meets weekly with his G-12 staff team while continuing to lead an open cell group.

The pastor was already meeting weekly with staff for planning and administration. Eventually the staff meeting was converted into a G-12 meeting. It began with prayer and ministry; then, they discussed the health of the cells under each pastor's care, and finally they hammered out various ministry details (see Chapter 4 for details about this type of meeting.)

This particular pastor decided that he also wanted to lead an open cell in his home on a different night because he was seeking to multiply leaders. I encouraged him not to become more concerned about his open cell—and the resulting new leaders—than with the staff prototype he was already developing.

Points to remember for a church this size:

- The senior pastor gathers his G-12 group by modeling cell life through a pilot cell.
- Staff members form part of the senior pastor's G-12 group.
- Each staff member must begin forming his or her own network of cells, while maintaining ministry responsibilities.
- Full-time staff members develop twelve cell leaders. Lay leaders gather groups of three (G-12.3.)

G-12.3 IN A LARGE CHURCH

The steps to develop G-12.3 in a large church normally follow the same steps used for a medium church, especially if the church is just beginning the transition to cell ministry:

- The senior pastor leads a pilot cell group with the staff members.
- Each staff member leads an open cell group.

- Each staff member develops a network of cells while continuing to be responsible for a particular ministry.
- The senior pastor meets weekly with his G-12 staff team while continuing to lead an open cell.

However, if the church already has a number of healthy small groups, you might want to use a different strategy. For example, I consulted with one large church of 3,500 that already had a dynamic cell ministry. The senior pastor, however, had delegated the position of 'cell minister' to an associate pastor.

Those pastors under this associate sensed an unspoken void because of the way the church was structured. They were reporting to one staff pastor who had the portfolio of cell ministry. The other staff pastors over the various ministries minded other matters (e.g., counseling, education, social action, missions, worship, administration, as well as the various age-related departments in the church.)

This church was ready for a change. The church knew that their present staff structure was not synchronized with an expanding cell system. The staff members asked hard questions, like, "How does the senior pastor fit into the cell structure?" and "How could other staff members become involved in cell ministry?" Here are my suggestions:

The senior pastor should assume the role of cell group minister.

I recommended that the senior pastor take on the role of cell group minister. He needed to begin leading an open cell group in order to model cell ministry for the rest of the church.

The senior pastor gathers a G-12 group.

Alongside his open cell group, the senior pastor took the place of cell minister by meeting weekly with his G-12 group. The former 'cell minister' and those under him reported directly to the senior pastor during the G-12 group meeting.

Each staff member leads an open cell group.

This was a revolutionary step. It stirred the leaders of the church to be on the playing field, rather than spectators in the stands.

Each staff member oversees a network of cells.

This particular church needed to shuffle some cells around so that each staff member could share the weight, although not every network needed to be the same size as the others. Some staff members were already so busy with their particular ministries that we thought it would be best to give them fewer cell groups in the beginning to oversee, allowing them to ease into the transition with the understanding that ministry loads would be adjusted in the future.

Eventually, each staff member's primary responsibility would be overseeing cell group leaders, although each one would also have a unique ministry assignment.

The senior pastor wrote to me six months later, "We've rearranged all our cells into networks and we have all our key staff and the former Area Pastors (lay leaders) leading cells this year—about 50 new cells in all. We've gone with a G-12.3 structure and it's looking really good."

Allow the homogeneous groupings to develop naturally.

A staff member might start out by leading his or her own cell. When the staff person multiplies his or her cell group, there will be two cell groups in the network (the mother cell and daughter cell.) The networks will grow naturally from there.

Allow lay people to become familiar with the G-12.3 structure.

Do not expect the congregation to make the cell church transition before the pastoral team does. Full-time staff members are called to wrestle with a wide variety of ministry-related issues. While many lay people are just as dedicated to the work of God, as a general rule, they have not worked through all of the philosophical issues of cell church ministry.

CONCLUSION

The G-12 phenomenon is worth understanding and applying. Just remember that you can learn and practice the precise methodology of ICM and fail miserably.

The reason is because you will need the creativity to adapt that ICM possesses. Claudia Castellanos says, "Those who have the power of the Spirit of God have the power of creativity."[1]

More than methods or models, we need God's creative power to inspire us to expect great things from God and to attempt great things for God.

Do you lack this power of creativity? It is easier to follow the creativity and trodden path of someone else. It requires less work. But your circumstances are unique. Only God knows the intimate details of your church. He has the "right fit" for your situation.

You will only find that "right fit" as you depend on the Holy Spirit. Do not copy the creativity of someone else. Allow the Spirit to give you fresh insight. Then follow that insight each day. Get the principles. Follow them and God Himself will sovereignly guide your steps.

APPENDIX:
SAMPLE G-12 LESSONS

SAMPLE ONE: SEVEN SECRETS OF EFFECTIVE LEADERS
JOHN MCMARTIN ~ LCLC G-12 MEETING

READ JOHN 10
Discuss Your Response to the Following Three Statements:

1. Leaders give people a sense of stability, hope and direction.
2. Leadership is learned.
3. Leading has great rewards—seeing people beginning to help and lead others, getting on with life.

Discuss ways in which we as leaders can implement the following *Seven Secrets of Effective Leaders* into our Cell Leadership.

Secret 1—Commitment.
- Long term commitment.
- As leaders we need to understand that if we chose not to actively lead our people someone or something else will. So many things beg their attention.

Secret 2—Know Well The Face Of Your Flock.
- Knowing how they are motivated or what discourages them.
- Know when they are struggling, when to back off, and when to push them harder.

Secret 3—Consistency.
- Meaning regular, predicable, and approachable.
- Keep your promises—never promise and not deliver.
- Guard your words.

Secret 4—Protecting.
- Adopt a healthy attitude to crisis—we can learn things from crisis.
- Get a good role model from whom you learn how to deal with crisis.
- Regain your confidence after a crisis by enjoying the support of other leaders.
- Understand your foundation—insecurity leaves you vulnerable to crisis.
- In times of crisis, talk with your friends.

Secret 5—Love the Church.
- Loving and speaking well of the church and its leadership will produce healthy, secure, confident disciples.

Secret 6—Be An Active Listener.
• Lots of voices—noise distracts, but listen to understand or listen in an understanding way and reflect back what you hear.

Secret 7—Be Equipped Spiritually.
• Read Ephesians 4:11-12; Deuteronomy 6:7; Romans 1:11.
• We impart of who we are and what we have.
• Let our equipping not be information only, but life.

SAMPLE TWO: How Jesus Developed Leaders
John McMartin ~ LCLC G-12 Meeting

• Jesus challenged people to follow him.
• Jesus said "follow me" 25 times in the gospels.
• Peter followed Christ to martyrdom.

• Peter—*1 Peter 2:21*
• Paul—*1 Corinthians 11:1*

• We are all called to follow Christ's example.
• Jesus took average people and transformed them into highly motivated leaders.

1. Jesus Called People Out Of The Crowd.
   • Jesus hand-picked the 12.
   • Jesus' objective—convert the crowd into disciples.
   • We must remember that our goal is to make disciples who will make disciples.

2. Jesus Taught And Demonstrated Vital Truths.

- Jesus not only taught on prayer—He demonstrated it (Luke 11:1-4).
- Jesus evangelized, and then instructed them afterwards.
- He took advantage of real life situations to explain doctrine (Matthew 19:23).
- Jesus constantly reviewed the experiences of His disciples, and then offered explanations.
- Mark 9:17-29
- Mark 6:30-44
- Give disciples experiences.
- Use experiences to teach lessons.
- Jesus married the theory to the practical.
- Mark 6:30; 10:17, 20
- People learn best by doing. However, they must not be left to themselves.
- They need personal supervision and guidance.

3. Jesus Focused On Future Leaders.

- Jesus knew that the transformation of the world would rest on men, not programs.
- Jesus even chose to flee from the crowd to concentrate on leaders who would become facilitators.
- Question: What's your ratio?
- Jesus did not neglect the crowd.
- Jesus took His disciples away from the crowd to teach them (Mark 9:30-31).
- The Book of Mark has 550 verses.
- 282 show Jesus relating to the public.
- 268 show Jesus working with the 12.

- The smaller the size of the group, the greater the possibility for instruction.
- Even out of the 12, Jesus narrowed his focus, first to Peter, James and John, and then just John.
- Teaching effectiveness coincides with group size.
- The crowd clamored for His attention.
     —John 16:15: take Him by force to make Him King.
     —John 12:19: Pharisees admitted that the crowd went after Him.
- Christ knew he had to concentrate on the few in order to prepare them to lead the multitude.
- Acts 2:41-42
- Jesus' strategy worked.
- Training must go past the classroom.
- An effective leader involves personal attention.

4. Jesus Demanded Obedience.

- Sometimes they failed to grasp the meaning of Christ' death on the cross (Matthew 16:22).
- They were often confused about their position (Mark 9:33-37).
- They were not keen on serving others (Matthew 20:24).
- Yet Jesus saw their teachable spirit/attitude and knew that they were willing to learn.
- Jesus disciples were willing to leave all and follow Him (Luke 5:11).
- This was a key ingredient—"Hold things very lightly."
- The characteristic of effective leaders today is obedience.
- Additional knowledge was only given as a result of acting upon what they knew.

5. Jesus Expected His Disciples To Reproduce.

- Christ's last command to His disciples clarifies the goal of His training (Matthew 28:19-20).

6. Following Christ's Pattern.

- The G-12.3 model gives us the perfect working model of training—teaching—doing.

Come On Let's Make Disciples!

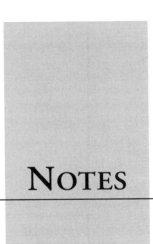

NOTES

INTRODUCTION

[1] David Oh, 28 February 2002, personal e-mail.

[2] David Oh, 28 February 2002, posted on cellchurchtalk, <http://www.cell-church.org/list/highlights.html>.

[3] As quoted by César Castellanos in César Castellanos and Claudia Castellanos, *Como Influir en Otros*, audiotape of conference in Bogota,Colombia, January 2002.

[4] As quoted in César Castellanos, *The Ladder of Success* (London: Dovewall Publications, 2001), preface to the UK edition.

[5] Many people cannot learn the G-12 system fully because they do not speak Spanish. As a missionary to Latin America, I have examined ICM from a more Latin American perspective. I have spoken to ICM's leaders, listened to the tapes and videos, and witnessed first-hand ICM's success. As we transitioned the Republic Church to the cell church model, using G-12 principles to guide us, we maintained close contact with ICM throughout the process.

[6] Rene Shelton, 12 August 2001, personal e-mail.

[7] Consider the distinctiveness of each church:

- A 53 year-old church with 80 in attendance (Sylmar, CA)
- A 70 year-old church with 25 in attendance (Los Angeles, CA)
- A 45 year-old church with 150 in attendance (Escondido, CA)
- An 86 year-old church with 300 in attendance (Chino, CA)
- A 60 year-old church with 100 in attendance (Redlands, CA)

[8] I am grateful to Pastor Rob Campbell, founder and senior pastor of Cypress Creek Church, for introducing me to the term 'team gathering.' Pastor Campbell uses a G-12 structure but has chosen to emphasize 'team' vocabulary because it fits better with the Texas culture.

CHAPTER 1

[1] Larry Stockstill, *Building Blocks of the Vision* (Baker, Louisiana: BCCN), audiotape of lecture presented at the International Cell Conference, November 2001.

[2] There are some differences between Bethany and ICM, although this might be simply because Bethany is still transitioning to the ICM model. For example, G-12 groups and cell groups are not separate at Bethany the way they are at ICM. Instead, Bethany asks new daughter cell leaders to return to their old cell groups for the G-12 meeting, thus making the original open cell both G-12 and evangelistic.

[3] Bethany grew from 491 cells in July 2001 to 816 cells in April 2002.

[4] Brad ?, June 1999, personal e-mail.

[5] At CCG, it takes approximately six months (two trimesters) before someone is allowed to lead a cell group.

[6] As of april 2002, the Metro Church International has approximately 25 men's cells, 50 women's cells, and 75 youth cells. The church holds Encounter weekends three times each month.

[7] José Rivas, *Carta Pastoral*, in the brochure for the Convencion Celular (March 2002), 23.

[8] Rocky Malloy, *Groups of Twelve: Launching Your Ministry into Explosive Growth* (Texas City, TX: Shield of Faith Ministries, 2002).
César Castellanos, *Leadership of Success through the Group of Twelve* (Bogota, Colombia: Vilit Editorial, 1999).

[9] Andreas Nuremburg, 13 August 2001, posted on cellchurchtalk. Andreas is a cell church planter in Germany.

[10] Larry Kreider, "Catching the Vision," *"Celebrating" CellChurch Magazine* (Houston, TX: TOUCH Publications, 2000), 23.

[11] Some people say that the new wineskin is the G-12 model, and the old wineskin is the cell church model. I believe that this is causing division. By following the basic principles, we can apply the best of G-12 to the cell church strategy, thereby promoting unity. The cell church strategy is much larger than a particular model (5x5, G-12, etc.)

[12] Some leaders in the G-12 movement teach that you must choose from the ICM model, the YFGC model, or Ralph Neighbour's model. They use the analogy of a Mercedes Benz: you cannot replace Mercedes Benz parts with the parts of a Honda. If you choose a Mercedes Benz, you must go with it completely. I believe a better analogy is the personal computer. IBM popularized it, but any company can make a clone or even improve it. We can use G-12 principles to radically improve the cell church. We do not need to buy a new model, just as it is not necessary to buy a new computer with a completely different operating system (like a Macintosh.)

[13] Mario Vega, senior pastor of the Elim Church, often sends me his statistical reports. The last one I received before sending this book to print was dated 10 October 2001.

GROWTH IN NUMBER OF CELLS
January 2001: 10,766
March 2001: 11,172
June 2001: 11,592
September 2001: 11,962

CELL ATTENDANCE
January 2001: 105,859
March 2001: 116,517
June 2001: 115,448
September 2001: 117,106

CONVERSIONS
As of September 2001: 9,905

BAPTIZED
As of September 2001: 4,295

CHAPTER 2

[1] There is some confusion over the term 'disciple' at ICM. Some say that a person can become a member of a G-12 even if he or she is not leading a cell group (and if that person does not bear fruit, he or she can be asked to leave.) Others say that a person cannot identify someone as part of his G-12 unless that person is leading a cell group. César Fajardo, famous youth pastor and now senior pastor at ICM, wrote to me saying, "It's clear that if someone isn't leading a cell group, he or she isn't a leader of anything and the G-12 groups are groups of leaders. Even though some at ICM are still fuzzy on this issue, I think it's far easier and helpful to say that a person is a 'disciple in progress' before the person is leading a cell (and just part of the normal evangelistic cell group) and when the person is leading a cell, that person becomes part of your G-12 group." This interpretation has been confirmed by those in Pastor César's inner circle, but because ICM is evolving so rapidly and constantly, not everyone is on the same page.

[2] Mike Osborn, 18 February 2002, personal e-mail.

[3] David Jaramillo, 19 February 2002, personal e-mail. David Jaramillo is the senior pastor of The Light Church in Quito, Ecuador. He began pastoring there in 1993. The average attendance for the previous 16 years was 120. Although he tried multiple programs, the church did not grow beyond 120 members. In 1999, Pastor Jaramillo began his transition to the cell church, and by 2002, the church has grown to 70 cell groups, 300 cell members, and 250 attending celebration services.

[4] Larry Stockstill, 21 February 2002, personal e-mail.

[5] LCLC does allow new G-12 leaders with only one person in the G-12 to combine with the parent G-12 until they have a second member. This is entirely optional and conditional on the fact that the parent leader also spends time with the new G-12 member.

[6] Andrew Harper, 7 March 2002, personal e-mail.

CHAPTER 3

[1] R.A.H. Gunner, "Number," in *New Bible Dictionary*, 2nd Ed., ed. J.D. Douglas, *et. al.* (Wheaton, IL: Tyndale, 1982), 845.

[2] David Brandon, 21 January 2002, personal e-mail.

[3] Steven L. Ogne, *Empowering Leaders through Coaching* (Carol Stream, IL: ChurchSmart Resources, 1995), audiotape.

[4] Billy Hornsby, *The Cell-Driven Church: Bringing in the Harvest* (Mansfield, PA: Fire Wind, 2000), 79.

CHAPTER 4

[1] Paul Yonggi Cho, *Successful Home Cell Groups* (Plainfield, NJ: Logos International, 1981), 107.

[2] Dale Galloway said this to a group of pastors at the Republic Church, 29 June 2000.

[3] As quoted in Brock and Bodie Thoene, *Writer to Writer* (Minneapolis, MN: Bethany House Publishers, 1990), 58.

[4] James C. Collins and Jerry I. Porras, *Built to Last: Successful Habits of Visionary Companies* (New York: HarperCollins Publishers, 1994), 173.

[5] Carl George, *Prepare Your Church for the Future* (Grand Rapids, MI: Fleming H. Revell, 1992), 60.

[6] Previously, each cell network provided ushers for one week of each month, but this system did not work well. We tried it for a year and a half. While it spread responsibility to many, our system was so unwieldly that it lacked organization. Our new method relies on one pastor to be responsible for this ministry, but every pastor is called on to provide the names of cell leaders who can serve in this capacity.

CHAPTER 5

[1] As quoted in Jay Firebaugh, *The Key is the Coach* (Houston, TX: TOUCH Publications, 1999), 9.

[2] Resources for coaches include Jay Firebaugh, *The Key is the Coach*, and Willow Creek Community Church's *Coaches Handbook*. Both provide great tips for effective coaching, but they will need to be adapted to the G-12.3 structure.

[3] The major headings were taken from Jay Firebaugh, *The Key is the Coach*. The material includes four audiotapes and a workbook.

CHAPTER 6

[1] Peter Wagner, *Churches that Pray* (Ventura, CA: Regal Books, 1993), 114.

[2] Ibid., 121.

[3] I recommend that every cell church has a cell information table. This table functions during the celebration service and provides the cell lessons, equipping track manuals, cell information (dates, times, locations), weekly cell reports, etc. A cell volunteer, preferably a cell leader, should be available at the table to answer questions. If your church has a cell secretary, he or she should be available during the Sunday worship services.

CHAPTER 7

1 César Fajardo, *The Vision*, audiotape of lecture presented at the Fourth Convention of Multiplication and Revival, January 1999.

2 Jonatan ?, 15 March 2001, personal e-mail. Jonatan is Pastor Obajah's son.

3 Lon Vining, 11 April 2001, posted on cellchurchtalk.

4 Mark Goodge, 20 June 2000, posted on cellchurchtalk.

5 According to my survey of over 700 cell leaders in 8 different countries, anyone, with any combination of gifts, can successfully lead a cell group and even multiply it.

6 Scott Boren, 30 June 2000, personal e-mail.

7 César Castellanos, *10 Commandments for Cell Group*, videotape of lecture presented at the ICM Conference in Bogota, Colombia, 1997.

8 Claudia Castellanos, cell seminar in Quito, Ecuador, May 1998.

9 César Castellanos, cell seminar in Quito, Ecuador, May 1998.

10 César Castellanos, *Sueña y Ganarás el Mundo* (Bogota, Colombia: Vilit Editorial, 1998), 174.

11 Tom Clegg and Warren Bird, "Lost in America: Helping Your Friends Find Their Way Home," *Journal for the American Society for Church Growth*, Spring (2001): 60.

CHAPTER 8

1 This concept is not new; ICM adapted the motto of Campus Crusade for Christ. My good friend, Ted Martin, one of the first on staff with Campus Crusade, told me, "When I came on CCC staff in 1960, there were two mottos on the wall in front of the chapel...one said, 'Win, Build, Send.' The other said, 'Win the Campus for Christ today, Win the World for Christ tomorrow.'"

2 Justin Mulder, 12 April 2001, posted on cellchurchtalk.

3 From Les Brickman, "Rapid Cell Church Growth and Reproduction: Case study of Eglise Protestante Baptiste Oeuvres et Mission Internationale, Abidjan, Cote D'Ivoire" (Ph.D. diss., Regent University, 2000).

4 Available for purchase at TOUCH Outreach Ministries. They best way to purchase these videos is by calling 1-800-735-5865 or 281-497-7901 Monday through Friday from 9 A.M. to 5 P.M. You can order my email: materials@touchusa.org or from TOUCH's website: www.touchusa.org, or by sending a fax to 281-497-0904.

5 Jim Egli, 16 January 2001, personal e-mail.

CHAPTER 9

1 One pastor's daughter introduced me to her G-12 group; it was composed primarily of male youth.

CHAPTER 11

1 César Castellanos, *Successful Leadership through the G-12 Model*, audiotape of lecture presented at the Fourth Convention of Multiplication and Revival, January 1999.

2 Actually, ICM teaches that you make your disciples into your image (César Castellanos, *Successful Leadership through the G-12 Model*, audiotape.) ICM will probably clarify this by saying that you make make your disciples to be like you because you are like Christ, which is biblical. Nevertheless, caution is in order.

CHAPTER 12

[1] I think it is a good idea to start a monthly Sunday or Saturday night celebration when there are three cells; Sunday or Saturday night celebrations every other week when there are five cells. When there are 7-10 cells, it is a good idea to start weekly celebration services.

CHAPTER 13

[1] A zone averages about 250 people in 25 cells. A district will number around 1,250 people in 125 cells. Understand that this is the ideal. I have observed that the 5x5 numbering is not always observed. Elim Church, for example, had eight zone pastors (as opposed to five) under each district pastor.

[2] In this particular church, we wrestled with the role of the children's pastor because she was hired to lead the Sunday school. We eventually agreed that she should be part of the pilot group with the goal of starting a children's cell. We did not think it was necessary for her to lead an adult cell since her primary ministry in the future would be to equip adults to lead children's cells. However, to equip well, she had to experience leading a children's cell herself.

CONCLUSION

[1] Claudia Castellanos, videotape of cell seminar in Quito, Ecuador, May 1998.

INDEX

ADDITIONAL RESOURCES
by Joel Comiskey

GROUPS OF 12

Finally, the definitive work that clears the confusion about the Groups of 12 model. Thousands of pastors have traveled to International Charismatic Mission to see it in operation. In this new title, Joel has dug deeply into ICM and other G-12 churches to learn the simple G-12 principles that can be transferred to your church. This book will contrast this new model from the classic structure and show you exactly what to do with this new model of cell ministry. 182 pgs.

REAP THE HARVEST

This book casts a vision for cell groups that will work in your church. Based on research of the best cell churches around the world and practical experience by the author, *Reap the Harvest* will reveal the 16 proven principles behind cell-church growth and effectiveness. It will also provide you with a strong biblical and historical foundation that anyone can understand. Great to share with key leaders as you transition to cell groups. 240 pgs.

HOME CELL GROUP EXPLOSION

This is the most researched and practical book ever written on cell-group ministry! Joel traveled the globe to find out why certain churches and small groups are successful in reaching the lost. He freely shares the answer within this volume. If you are a pastor or a small group leader, you should devour this book! It will encourage you and give you simple, practical steps for dynamic small group life and growth. 152 pgs.

HOME CELL GROUP EXPLOSION STUDY GUIDE

This companion study guide has been developed to enhance and propel both current and future leaders in their ministry. It will help you learn and apply the practices of successful cell leaders. You can use this guide privately, in a small group setting or in cell leader training sessions. 36 pgs.

LEADERSHIP EXPLOSION

Cell Groups are leader breeders. Yet few churches have enough cell leaders ready to start new groups. In this book, you will discover the leadership development models used by churches that consistently multiply leaders. Then you will learn how to create your own model that will breed leaders in your church. 208 pgs.

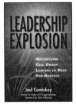

Order Toll-Free from TOUCH Outreach Ministries
1-800-735-5865 • Order Online: www.touchusa.org

CELL GROUP LEADER TRAINING RESOURCES

CELL GROUP LEADER TRAINING:
Leadership Foundations for Groups that Work,
by Scott Boren and Don Tillman

The Trainer's Guide and Participant's Manual parallel the teaching of Comiskey's *How to Lead a Great Cell Group Meeting.* Through the use of teaching, creative activities, small group interaction, and suggested between-the-training exercises, this eight-session training will prepare people for cell group leadership like no other tool. The Trainer's Guide provides teaching outlines for all eight sessions and options for organizing the training, including different weekly options and retreat options. The Trainer's Guide also has bonus sections, including teaching outlines for the *Upward, Inward, Outward, Forward* Seminar and detailed interview discussion guides for *The Journey Guide for Cell Group Leaders.* This comprehensive training tool will establish your group leaders on a sure foundation.

HOW TO LEAD A GREAT CELL GROUP MEETING...
...So People Want to Come Back,
by Joel Comiskey

Joel Comiskey takes you beyond theory and into the "practical tips of the trade" that will make your cell group gathering vibrant! This hands-on guide covers all you need to know, from basic how-to's of getting the conversation started to practical strategies for dynamic ministry times. If you're looking to find out what really makes a cell group meeting great...this book has the answers! 144 pgs.

8 HABITS OF EFFECTIVE SMALL GROUP LEADERS,
by Dave Earley

Are your cell leaders truly effective in changing lives? They can be! After years of leading and overseeing growing small groups, Pastor Dave Earley has identified 8 core habits of effective leaders. When adopted, these habits will transform your leadership too. The habits include: Dreaming • Prayer • Invitations • Contact Preparation • Mentoring • Fellowship • Growth. When your leaders adopt and practice these habits, your groups will move from once-a-week meetings to an exciting lifestyle of ministry to one another and the lost! 144 pgs.

LEADING FROM THE HEART,
by Michael Mack

Recharge your cell leadership! Powerful cell leaders share a common trait: a passionate heart for God. They know their priorities and know that time with Him is always at the top of the list. Do your cell leaders attract others? Is their cell ministry central to their lives? This book will renew their hearts, refocus their priorities and recharge their ministry. If you have a sense that your leaders are tired of ministry or frustrated with people, this title will help! And, if your leaders have great attitudes and you want to help them move to the next level, this book will move them into new fields, white for harvest! 152 pgs.

ADDITIONAL CELL GROUP LEADER RESOURCES

UPWARD, INWARD, OUTWARD, FORWARD WORKBOOK
Improving the 4 Dynamics of Your Cell Group,
by Jim Egli

This easy to use workbook, combined with the facilitator's presentation (Part 2 of this Guide) will help your cell groups grow in the four basic dynamics of healthy cell life. Upward: Deepening your relationship to the Father; Inward: Deepening community between cell members; Outward: Reaching the lost for Jesus successfully; Forward: Developing and releasing new leaders. 72 pgs (Participant's Guide.)

THE JOURNEY GUIDE FOR CELL GROUP LEADERS

This tool will help your interns and cell leaders evaluate their leadership abilities and determine their next steps toward effective group leadership. It will help you as a pastor or trainer identify the needs of your future or current leaders so that you can better train and mentor them.

303 ICE BREAKERS:
At last...303 ways to really "BREAK THE ICE" in your cell group!

You will never need another icebreaker book. This collection places at your fingertips easy-to-find ideas divided into nine categories, such as "Including the Children," "When a Visitor Arrives" and "Lighthearted and Fun." This is a needed reference for every cell meeting. We've included instructions on how to lead this part of the meeting effectively. 156 pgs.

OUR BLESSING LIST POSTER

Growing cell churches have proven that constant prayer for the lost yields incredible results! Use this nifty poster to list the names of your your friends who do not know Christ and pray for them every time you meet. 34" x 22", folds down to 8.5" x 11" and comes with a handout master, equipping track and a master prayer list. Pack of 10.

ARE YOU FISHING WITH A NET?,
by Randall G. Neighbour

Lead your group into team evangelism. These proven steps will prepare your members to reach out effectively as a group. 12 pgs.

Order Toll-Free from TOUCH Outreach Ministries
1-800-735-5865 • Order Online: www.touchusa.org

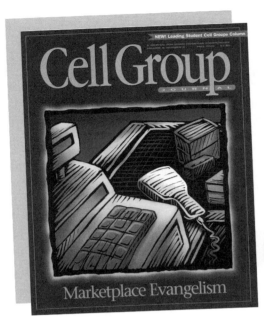

ENCOUNTER GOD!

What is Encounter God?

A simple, easy-to-use weekend resource to help you walk your church through a spiritual freedom experience.

• *Encounter God* remains effective when used with large groups of people, saving precious time.
• *Encounter God* is both a truth and power encounter.

Why Encounter God?

Spiritual strongholds in the life of a Christian are dark areas of bitterness, unforgiveness and secret sin that keep him from seeing his own worth, leadership potential and purpose in life. If your church members resist discipleship, and/or have no passion for the lost, a spiritual freedom weekend experience will help them see areas of their heart where they need healing and give them a safe environment to receive ministry. *Encounter God* is also a wonderful tool for helping new converts overcome old flesh patterns and beginning their new walk with increased spiritual freedom.

Believers who are set free from the grip of sinful habits and attitudes enjoy a fruitful, purpose-filled life!

I'm using another ministry's resources. Why change?

• Facilitating *Encounter God* doesn't require a counseling degree, and is easily transferred to others.
• *Encounter God* builds your church's ministry and vision…not a parachurch organization.
• *Encounter God* will release your church to reach the lost, disciple others and bring them through the spiritual freedom process.
• *Encounter God* is adaptable, and can be used in a variety of ways in all kinds of church settings.

How does Encounter God work?

You will present a series of large group teaching times, followed by one-on-one ministry by the participants, who are paired up for the event. The participants will learn how to minister to another person effectively and hold each other accountable after the event, as well as share from their own hearts and find spiritual freedom from satanic strongholds.

How much preparation is required?

The materials we have designed make preparation as easy as possible! *The Instructor's Guide* is very clear on how to present the materials yourself or use the video. *The Video Series* contains seven hours of professionally created sessions that you can use to prepare or show during the actual retreat. *The Retreat Guide* will help you choose a good location, select from a variety of possible schedules, and answer frequently asked questions.

Who can facilitate this weekend?

Any spiritually mature man and woman can do this (the man and woman do not have to be married, but it does enhance the weekend if they are). We suggest that the senior pastor and his wife facilitate the first one so that they can testify to its power and effectiveness.

ADDITIONAL RESOURCES ON CELLS

WHERE DO WE GO FROM HERE?
THE 10TH ANNIVERSARY EDITION,
by Ralph W. Neighbour, Jr.

With updated data on new cell church models, new information on equipping and harvest events and practical teaching on how to begin a transition, this book will continue to stir hearts to dream about what the church can be. You will find hope for the church in North America and discover the new things that Dr. Neighbour has learned over the last 10 years. Share this vision with a friend. 400 pgs.

THE SECOND REFORMATION,
by William A. Beckham

Don't jump head-first into a cell church transition or church plant without reading this book! Beckham brilliantly walks you through the logic of a cell/celebration structure from a biblical and historical perspective. He provides you with a step-by-step strategy for launching your first cells. This wonderful companion to Neighbour's material will ground you in the values and vision necessary for a successful transition to cells. 253 pgs.

LIFE IN HIS BODY,
by David Finnell

Communicate the vision of the cells to everyone in your church with this simple tool. The short chapters followed by discussion questions clearly define cell life for your leaders and members so that they can catch a lifestyle of prayer, community and evangelism. This book will give your church hope and vision as your members discover the possibilities of the New Testament community. 160 pgs.

SHEPHERD'S GUIDEBOOK,
by Ralph W. Neighbour, Jr.

This thoroughly tested book will equip your cell leaders for success and train them to listen to God for their cell members, develop community and lead people into relationship evangelism. Not only will your cell leaders gain the tools for leading a cell meeting, they will also learn to pastor their flocks and multiply the ministry of your church. 256 pgs.

Order Toll-Free from TOUCH Outreach Ministries
1-800-735-5865 • Order Online: www.touchusa.org